CLINKER PLYWOOD
BOATBUILDING
MANUAL

IAIN OUGHTRED

A WoodenBoat Book

Published by WoodenBoat Publications, Inc
Naskeag Road, PO Box 78
Brooklin, Maine 04616 USA
www.woodenboat.com

ISBN: 0-937822-61-2

Copyright 2004
Iain Oughtred
Struan Cottage
Bernisdale, Isle of Skye
Scotland IV51 9NS

First published 1988 in Scotland

Book Design: Posthouse Printing & Publishing,
Findhorn Bay, Scotland +44 (0)1309691640/1

Cover Design: Sally Elizabeth Bowen

Front cover image: Ness Yawl Jeanie Henderson

Printed in Canada by Friesens

THE AUTHOR

After a successful career in centreboard
racing dinghies, Iain Oughtred became one of
the leading lights of the British wooden boat
revival, designing, building and sailing many
remarkable craft. These boats have gained a
world-wide reputation for their elegance of
line, sound construction, and excellent sailing
performance. His perfectionist approach may
be unbusinesslike, but provides highly refined
designs and detailed plans. In this he hopes to
encourage a return to a deep appreciation of
traditional values of craftsmanship, believing
this is a vital part of the true education, and
thus helps to nourish the human spirit in an
impoverished age.

15ft Faering Elf   photo by Kathy Mans

ACKNOWLEDGEMENTS

My grateful thanks are due to several good friends, without whom this work would have been less than it is:

Sveinung Skatun and Betsy got me tied down in front of a computer and introduced me to 20th century technology. Topher Dawson, Brice Avery, and John Lowe read the manuscript and helped to rationalize some of the sillier ideas. Simon Bowen has done an excellent job on the design and layout.

The work of several of our best boat-builders is illustrated in these pages, including Anton Fitzpatrick, Jamie Clay, Jack Chippendale, Topher Dawson, David Mitchell, Robert Angus with Martin, and Rae Smith. Amateur builders who provided necessary photographs of their successful projects include Ian Borthwick, Terry Pullen, Mike Greenway, David Merryweather, and others too numerous to mention.

The helpful hands of Mike Hall, Mary F, Gandolf, and John Lowe also appear.

bundin er båtlaus madur
bound is boatless man

Viking proverb

Contents

Contents

Fitting Out

Chapter 7:

Chapter 8:

1-1

'Every journey begins with a single step', and boatbuilding is, after all, a matter of cutting out pieces of wood and putting them together. Time spent studying the plans before beginning is time well spent; the mists of confusion will gradually clear.

For those who do find the prospect of building and fitting out a whole boat is too much to contemplate, or simply do not have the time available, compromises may be considered. Professional boatbuilders can build a bare hull, or a hull plus spars, or, as in the case of this Ness Yawl, Fig 1-1, a shell with perhaps centreboard case and bulkheads. (The finished boat may be seen in Figs 6-167 and 168).

I have to confess that practically all of the boats illustrated are designs from my own catalogue of stock plans. My excuses for this are: nearly all the photographs I have to work with are of these boats. Most of the construction methods and details have been worked out and refined in the building of them, and they represent 'state of the art' construction. Finally, the range of designs covers the whole spectrum of hull types, from simple flat-bottom prams, through dories and the three-strake-a-side double-enders, up to full round-bilge hulls and even small cruising yachts. We will be taking a look at the different basic hull types a little later.

The methods shown may generally be applied to boats by other designers, although they should be consulted before significant changes are made. Other designs found in books and magazines may be built this way, provided that a contemporary designer's copyright does not apply. You may need to do some research however before deciding on scantlings etc.

Many of the functions of small craft have changed little over time, and their shapes and proportions have gradually evolved. As for construction methods, however, the last fifty years have seen changes more revolutionary than had occurred for many centuries. Using contemporary technology, designers of recreational craft are aiming for lighter hulls, easier handling, better windward performance, and lower maintenance than their predecessors were generally able to achieve. These qualities are more relevant to recreational sailors than they were to fishermen.

Glued-lap plywood is one of the most attractive, efficient, and economical methods of boatbuilding. It lends itself to a wide range of designs - traditional and modern, simple and sophisticated - and builders of all levels of skill and experience. As the name implies, the method relies not on mechanical fastenings, but rather glued plank seams.

The intention of this book is to describe and to illustrate in detail the procedures involved in building clinker plywood boats of varying types and sizes. I am well aware that many first-time boatbuilders must find it an intimidating experience to unfold a set of plans - or even perhaps to skim through this book. It can all look very complicated. But

1-2 WHY CLINKER?

The stiffness of wood along its grain makes it difficult for the builder to force it into extreme bends; with no rigid frames to create hard spots, the hull can hardly help but come out fair. One of the beauties, aesthetically and functionally, of clinker boats is the way the strakes closely follow the lines of water flow along the hull. It may be that the water is encouraged by these ridges along the hull to conform to these easy flow lines, thereby steadying the hull in its forward motion. Fig 1-2.

Compared with a smooth-skinned hull, lapstrake boats have an obvious increase in wetted surface and some turbulence along the laps, but these do not seem to have a noticeably negative effect on performance, even in light racing boats, where it would quickly be apparent. The laps also help to knock down spray, so the boat will be drier; they inhibit rolling, and they slightly increase lateral resistance and directional stability. The clinker boat is better behaved.

1-3 WHY PLYWOOD?

Also, the inherent strength of lapstrake construction, when combined with plywood and modern adhesives, eliminates the need for frames. The result is essentially a strong, monocoque, single-skinned hull with a pleasing traditional appearance. The interior structure is simpler, and thus easier to build and to maintain. Fig 1-3.

For some purposes, solid clinker planking fastened with copper rivets may still be best. For example, some builders feel that the substantial planks of a heavier clinker boat that will be hauled up and down a gravelly beach stand abuse better than thin plywood veneers (although hardwood strips glued over the plywood edges can offer protection). However, a hire fleet owner reports that although he has had to replace practically every part of many of his boats' hulls, including stems, keels and transoms, the plywood planking remains sound after over thirty years of service.

Some builders may like to build a traditional boat for the challenge of doing it the old-fashioned way. For most purposes, however, the substitution of plywood and glue for solid planks, frames and rivets is well worth consideration.

The advantages are:

- Marine plywood is readily available.
- Plywood is consistent and dependable in quality, and even in thickness.
- Plywood is easier to find than planking stock, and comes ready for use.
- When glued, the plywood planking will not work, split or leak.
- Plywood is far less affected than solid planking by variations in temperature and humidity; a lapstrake plywood boat can be transported overland in hot weather without opening up.
- The clean interior of a lapstrake plywood hull is far easier to maintain than that of a framed-out hull.
- Lapstrake plywood hulls are, usually, considerably lighter in weight than traditional clinker boats.
- Plywood construction is an economical choice.
- Many of the traditional skills and specialized equipment of the old-time boatshop are not necessary. (It is wonderfully encouraging that many people are now learning and using these skills, but for many amateurs with limited time and resources it is hardly feasible).
- It makes a good-looking boat, with a traditional style.

DESIGN

1-4

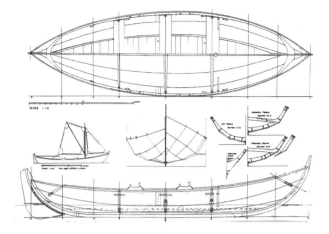

The selection of a design will depend on many considerations - not all of them entirely rational. You may be fascinated with the shape and style of a particular type of boat, and will not be satisfied until you have built one. Or you may be the sensible type who knows exactly what a boat is needed for, and finds the most practical design for the purpose. Or, more than likely, a combination of both.

You're in luck if your ideal design can be found among the stock plans of a designer who specializes in boats for amateur boatbuilders. Especially if he is one who builds and sails the boats himself. Whether or not the design is a traditional one, or an adaptation, or a modern design, he will have done all the hard work of suiting the boat to its intended purpose, working out a construction system which is suitable for inexperienced builders, and is strong enough for the many and varied stresses it may encounter in use, without being heavier than necessary.

He should be able to provide a set of full size patterns for the moulds, stem and transom, which will save you the trouble of having to loft the lines full size. (Some plans come with computer-generated mould and plank patterns, but these seem to have a reputation for being unpredictable, and occasionally wildly inaccurate).

If you are interested in a straight traditional type of boat, you will find that some craft are more suitable than others for recreational use. The more lightly built river skiffs, canoes etc adapt well to clinker plywood, and make good use of its qualities of light weight and transportability. These types after all were generally built as recreational boats. Traditional scantlings may be close to ideal, except that the steamed ribs may be eliminated, and generally the thickness of the planking stock may be reduced.

A traditional workboat type may originally have been more heavily built. Provided that the displacement at the LWL - the designed waterline - is not too great, it may be feasible to lighten up the structure considerably. But a light hull, built to the original full-bodied load-carrying shape, may float very high in the water, becoming unstable unless ballasted, and/or needing a reduction in freeboard. But drastic redesigning is not to be undertaken lightly.

If a traditional design is selected, the builder may have little more to work from than a lines plan, probably at a very small scale, hopefully with a table of offsets, and some basic information about the construction: Fig 1-4. In this case the lines will need to be laid down full size, in order to find the exact shape of the moulds, stem and transom. This will also be useful in working out the shapes and sizes of many other parts.

Or you may feel inspired by a particularly elegant example of an old boat, with no plans existing; many after all were built by eye with no drawings at all. You can then, if you have the time and patience, take off the lines (see WoodenBoat no. 107) and take detailed notes and dimensions and preferably photographs of all parts of the hull. (No you can not build her by eye! - not unless you have learned how to do it through generations of boatbuilder ancestors. It takes no more time to build a well-modeled hull than a bad one).

Another method of reproducing an old clinker boat, if she is still the right shape - not hogged or twisted, and roughly the same both sides - is to make up a set of moulds which are spiled and shaped to fit into the existing hull at suitable station points. This will not give you a set of lines, but you get the hull shape, and the planks all lined out exactly as in the old boat.

If you are still undecided about what type of hull to go for, it may be useful here to take a brief look at the various basic hull shapes.

FLAT-BOTTOMED SKIFFS AND DORIES

1-5

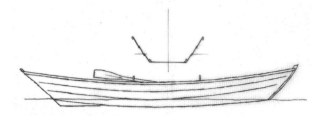

Although they are not clinker boats in the usual sense, a type which deserves at least a brief mention is the dory-style, flat bottom, flat sided hull; an example is the Mackerel Dory - Fig 1-5. A 'light dory', the topsides may be built from a single panel; however the three lapstrake planks give a more traditional style, reminiscent of the Banks dories.

1-6

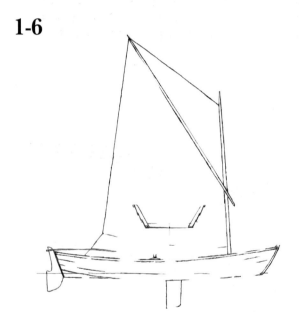

The Seahorse Skiff - Fig 1-6 - is built the same way. To row well, flatties must be narrow on the waterline; to carry sail with assurance, they need more beam. So a compromise must be found; in general sailing flatties will pound and slap in choppy water and be limited to sheltered areas. Wide flat surfaces are generally avoided in the design of seagoing craft; rounder shapes are lighter and stiffer and offer less resistance. But, the flatties do have an appealing air of functional simplicity. The flat surface areas require some internal framing, or heavier plywood planking to achieve sufficient stiffness, and chine logs are needed, except perhaps in the smaller and lighter boats - under about 12' - 3 - 3.5m overall.

The parts may be simpler in shape, but there are usually more parts to fit together than a true clinker hull needs. Although these traditional skiffs work well within their limitations, and many owners are well pleased with them, I believe - and hope to demonstrate - that a more able boat can be built just as easily.

DORY SKIFF

1-7

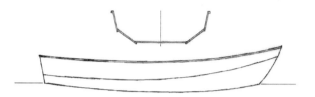

Here - in Fig 1-7 - we have what may be about the ultimate in functional simplicity in a small - 11 or 12'-3.5m - general purpose boat. A kind of 'minimalist' lapstrake. The hull is an attempt to design the ideal combination rowing/sailing/outboard boat, which can be built in a minimum amount of time.

1-8

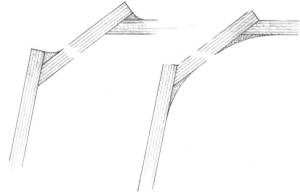

The narrower bottom panel may be lighter, or need less framing, than the flat skiff. The sharp angle of the chines reduces the width of the lands where the planks overlap; the lands must therefore be backed up with epoxy fillets, outside and perhaps inside also, as seen in the two optional methods in Fig 1-8. If other glues are used, the fillets are replaced by wood strips.

A larger hull may have three or more strakes to a side, as seen in the round-sided prams below.

This is the kind of hull shape that is often built by the stitch-and-tape method.

Aside from eliminating the fibreglass tape, glued clinker differs in that the plank edges must be bevelled. This requires a sharp plane and a reasonable ability to handle it. Epoxy however offers a great degree of gap-filling forgiveness for imperfect joints; close fits are not necessary at all.

ROUND SIDED PRAMS

1-9

WoodenBoat's Nutshell Pram, designed by Joel White, is probably the best known example of this type. The design is unusual in that it has a vee-bottom shape forward. This works very well in choppy water, but it requires a laminated stem, which complicates the structure.

1-10

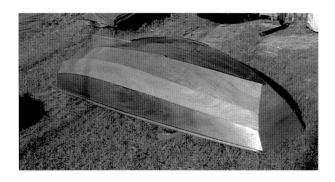

The Mouse Pram shown in Figs 1-9 and 10 has a flat bottom that simply comes through to the bow transom. This is the simplest form of proper lapstrake planking. It makes an interesting comparison with the popular 'stitch-and-tape' seam construction. Stitch and tape requires less skill and care in fitting the parts together, but can take considerably more time, with all the stitching, taping and filling. And it generally precludes a bright finish.

1-11

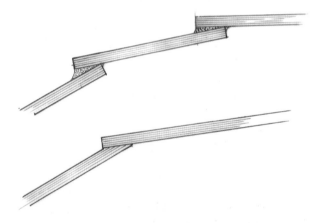

Some lapstrake kit boats use a greater number of strakes to reduce the angle at each lap, and do without bevelling altogether. This leaves a wide gap under the lower edge of each lap, except in areas where the planks are nearly parallel; this makes the plank appear much thicker than it actually is. As the comparison of the two joints in Fig 1-11 shows, it can sometimes look a little amateurish, but it demonstrates the ability of epoxy resin to keep the water out, and to hold the hull together.

Precise bevels and neat fits all round may bring the builder some satisfaction, but are structurally irrelevant, if using epoxy. This does not apply, however, when using other glues.

Introduction

ROUND-SIDED DORY CONSTRUCTION

1-12

This is basically the same system as used for the round sided prams, with the addition of a stem. In light dories, for example the Amberjack Dory shown in Fig. 1-12, the extra buoyancy provided by the rounded topsides adds some useful reserve stability, which enhances her ability under sail, while retaining the narrow bottom for low resistance and fast rowing.

1-13

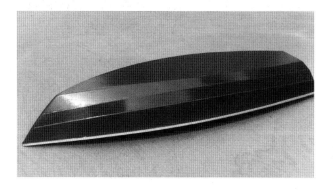

This is an ideal construction method for home-buildable multi-purpose boats. It works well in a beamier dory-skiff hull; Fig 1-13 shows a semi-planing hull which will row moderately well, and will also be quite fast and stable under sail or with outboard power.

Building a hull of this type is almost as easy as building a pram. The flat bottom eliminates the need for a keel, there is a minimum number of strakes, and there is not much twist in any of them. The stem is usually sawn in one piece, maybe with a protective outer stem added after planking. This method lends itself well to efficient and economical kit production.

VEE-BOTTOM HULLS

1-14

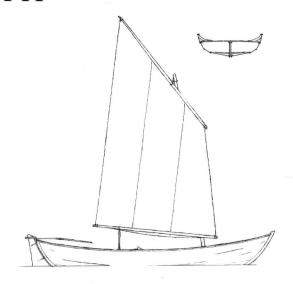

Here we have the addition of a keel, which, while it complicates the procedure a little, allows for a more sophisticated hull shape. However, the hull still has relatively few parts; about half the number that go into a traditional single- or double-chine plywood boat, which until fairly recently was regarded as the ultimate in home-built simplicity.

John Watkinson pioneered this type of construction with his Drascombe Lugger. With this design he showed that the structure could be greatly simplified by eliminating the usual chine stringers, and using very little framing. The early boats were glued with resorcinol, and even if neglected seemed to stay together indefinitely.

The Ness Yawl in Fig 1-14 is an example of a traditionally inspired design that can be successfully transmuted into lapstrake plywood construction. She becomes a somewhat different kind of boat, far more useful for recreational sailing but still embodying much of the character of the original Shetland type.

In building the vee-bottomed hulls, the keelson is set up over the temporary moulds and glued to the stems, or stem and transom.

The wide garboard or bottom panels require a changing bevel right along the keelson and will be twisted around the forefoot. Thereafter the planking proceeds in the same way as in typical dory construction.

TRADITIONAL PRAMS

1-15

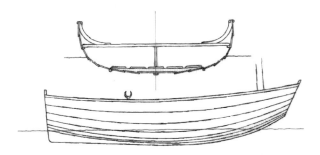

Now we have progressed to fully planked, round-bilged clinker. A small pram is a good way to start with this construction, whether it is in solid or plywood planking. The bottom is usually flat; most often it is made in one wide strake, twice the width of a normal plank, with a light external keel fitted after planking. The pram bow makes the planking process considerably easier, as there is very little twist in any of the strakes.

One way in which the use of plywood can affect the design of a round-bilge boat is that fewer strakes are necessary. With one third or two fifths - depending on the number of veneers - of the grain going across the plank, there is considerable extra strength perpendicular to the run of the planking, which virtually eliminates the possibility of splitting, and so wider strakes are quite feasible.

Typically, the Humble Bee Pram in Fig 1-15 has ten strakes a side in her traditional version, and eight in plywood. Technically speaking, five or six plywood strakes would be quite sufficient, but part of the purpose of the design is to look traditional. (These boats are often built traditionally also).

CANOES

1-16

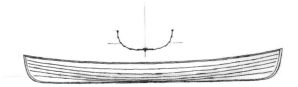

A small open canoe, like the Wee Lassie type in Fig 1-16, can easily be built to weigh less than 20 lbs / 9kg. The planking may be very light - 1/8" - 3 to 4mm. A canoe's hull is more complex than that of a pram, but the light materials are so easy to handle that it is almost nearer to modelmaking than boatbuilding.

Larger cruising canoes are often half-decked. Plywood is particularly good for decks and bulkheads, especially when combined with epoxy fillets. This gives a strong light job in a lot less time than it takes to fit little backing cleats all around the hull sides.

TRADITIONAL PULLING BOATS, DINGHIES, AND SKIFFS.

1-17

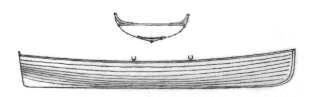

This is the real thing. The classification includes such types as clinker yacht tenders, fast pulling boats and launches, as well as traditional craft like canoe yawls, lapstrake Whitehalls, and the Acorn Skiffs - Figs 1-3 and 17.

The basic hull structure consists of the backbone, planking, floors, and gunwale assembly. As with the prams and canoes, building these hulls with the glued-lap method will probably require one or two fewer strakes per side than traditional construction.

DAYSAILERS

1-18

BIGGER BOATS?

1-19

Boats of this type are generally beamier than most of the above boats, and have varying degrees of traditional character. Some designs use quite wide strakes; some even combine the lower two or three strakes into one plywood panel - like the wide vee-bottom form of the double-enders we looked at earlier. In most cases there will be some decking and built-in buoyancy. The Gannet, shown in Fig 1-18, is a typical lapstrake dayboat or sailing dinghy. Again, epoxy filleting methods are very useful in the fitting of plywood bulkheads and decks. But, not essential, I should keep repeating, for the benefit of those who prefer conventional glues to epoxy.

If the sailing rig involves standing rigging, consideration must be given to the compression forces set up by the shrouds and forestay. These stresses will be trying to push the mast down through the bottom of the boat, with an equivalent upward force at the chainplates.

Right before the advent of fibreglass devastated the boatbuilding industry, there were some very appealing small cruising yachts and cruiser-racers built in clinker plywood. Jack Laurent Giles's tiny sloop Sopranino demonstrated the potential of this method on her transAtlantic cruise; if proof were needed John Guzzwell's fattened-up version sailed around the world. Illingworth and Primrose designed a number of successful JOG racers; several designers in Holland produced some very attractive cruisers. Perhaps the best-known is van der Stadt's Waarschip - Fig 1-19 - which was available in kit form in the early 1970s. With her generous beam and freeboard, a good-sized cabin, and conventional sloop rig, she was a very normal small yacht of her time. But, with a well-proportioned hull and lapstrake sides, she looked better than most - then and now. An updated version is still built in Holland.

With wide bottom and topside panels, and four 'chines' making three lapped strakes around the turn of the bilge, the hull shape is actually a compromise between chine plywood and a round-bilge shape, incorporating the best qualities of both. Although externally the hull resembles the vee-bottom type described above, (Fig 1-14), the structure is relatively complex, with full frames, and a stringer at each plank land. Although these stringers make it easy to fasten the planks, there is quite a bit of work to be done in fitting them and planing the bevels. This work can be done efficiently in a production setup; if fibreglass had not happened when it did, boats like these would have been produced in large numbers worldwide.

1-20

The well-known Folkboat is a good example of a conventional clinker boat that has been successfully built in plywood. The smaller Grey Seal - Fig 1-20 - which was specifically designed for plywood, is another. Her planking is 1/2"/12mm plywood on laminated frames, which add great strength and make serious offshore cruising feasible. The hull is built upside-down, as are the smaller boats, and the frames are temporarily fastened to moulds.

So far, not many boatbuilders seem willing to construct larger boats using clinker plywood, for no apparent reason other than convention. Historically, clinker planked ships were limited in size by the degree of flexibility inherent in their construction. Beyond a certain length - variable according to beam, displacement etc - unfair stresses are concentrated on plank and scarph fastenings. So eventually the builders of larger trading vessels went for the more rigid, heavier-framed carvel method. These days, lapstrake boats are not often seen exceeding about 30'-10m overall; most are under 20' - 6.5m. (The ancient Scandinavian belief in the desirability of a flexible hull can still be seen however in the sparsely-framed faerings and Shetland yoles).

This size limitation seems, in practice, to apply to glued plywood hulls as well. However, the elimination of mechanical fastenings and slight working between the strakes mean there is no practical reason why larger boats can not be built using lapstrake plywood. Except perhaps that the standard length of a sheet of plywood is 8' - 2440mm - occasionally 10' - 3m - and this means that many scarph joins are needed to build a longer boat. Some factories have scarphing machinery that can turn out sheets of infinite length, but this is rare now that nearly all plywood is imported. Simple accurate jigs can be made, however, which, when combined with an efficient gluing setup and ample space, allow the operation to be done quite quickly. Such a jig is shown in Part 5.

The exposed edges of the plywood seem vulnerable, but can easily be protected with hardwood strips glued to the underside of each strake.

Introduction

CHAPTER 2

TOOLS & MATERIALS

WOOD

2-1

Selection of hull materials will depend mainly on what is locally available. Boat construction requires top quality wood, so be prepared to spend a lot of time if necessary looking through piles of stuff, looking for good clear straight-grained boards. Yard men and managers are generally patient, and respect a craftsman's need for high quality materials. (In return they deserve consideration for their limited time).

HARDWOOD

Some of the hardwood species most used in boatbuilding are:

MAHOGANY - most readily available species are hardly up to boatbuilding quality. But Brazilian mahogany is excellent, being

strong and durable, and looks good when bright finished. Top end of 'medium' weight scale.

KHAYA - a popular medium-weight mahogany, consistent in quality; available also as veneer for cold-moulding and as plywood.

OAK - hard and strong; rather heavy for extensive use in lighter boats. Excellent for rubbing strakes, cleats etc. Oak seems to have a reputation for not gluing well, but some tests I did with epoxy indicated that this may not be justified. One or two joints with smooth-planed oak proved to be not quite as strong as the wood itself; for a short distance the joint failed along the glue line. But all samples were OK when the wood was sanded across the grain with coarse paper before gluing.

ASH - moderately heavy; very tough and flexible. Not durable, so not much used for backbones, floors etc. American white ash is straight, clear and white. European ash is harder to find in good straight lengths; often has areas of olive/brown colour. Ash is traditionally often used for steamed ribs in light canoes and skiffs; it is excellent for oars, when weight is not a primary consideration. When bright finished, ash quickly turns grey and weathered looking when the surface finish is worn and the wood exposed.

IROKO - hard, strong, heavy, durable. Used a substitute for teak; not quite the same quality appearance, but stronger. A pungent peppery smell when sawn. Irregular grain can cause twisting. Used for backbone structure in larger boats.

WYCH ELM - medium weight; durable. I like to use a lot of elm, finding it an excellent substitute for mahogany etc. Quality varies; good stuff is tough, works and glues well and looks very good when bright finished. In some areas of Britain there is still quite a lot available after the onslaught of Dutch Elm disease; the wood itself is unaffected. (English elm is less useful, having a wild wavy grain; the mainly Scottish Wych Elm withstands the disease much better, and so continues to be available). Canadian rock elm is a superb boat-building wood, but is now rare (its import is banned in Britain since the disease struck, although it is unaffected by it).

AGBA - a good all-round timber, light for a hardwood and durable.

AFRORMOSIA - hard, heavy and durable. Another teak substitute, but generally stronger. Takes a fine finish; used for high-class joinery.

BURMA TEAK - now very rare and very expensive, teak is not particularly strong for its weight, but is a fine looking wood and is extraordinarily durable.

Any of these woods can be used for the basic structural members, although the harder ones are more demanding to work and require extra care in gluing.

The official durability rating of any species is less significant than the way the boat is built, used, and maintained, especially with small craft which are less likely to be left afloat. The use of epoxy coating or sheathing can raise the effective durability rating a notch or two, by isolating the wood from the elements.

SOFTWOOD

DOUGLAS FIR - medium weight, strong and resilient. An excellent all-round material, available in long clear lengths, which can be used for all parts of a lighter boat, and is very good for spars.

AMERICAN YELLOW PINE - generally available. A very good substitute for fir. Similar in appearance, but lighter in colour. Moderately durable.

LARCH - is a good tough and durable wood, traditionally used for clinker planking. But rare in slow-grown 'boatskin' quality; often very knotty. Often used in plywood boats for thwarts, bottom boards etc.

CENTRAL AMERICAN PITCH PINE - lighter than old pitchpine, but strong and very durable. Available in large sizes.

PITCHPINE - the old pitchpine, only available now from old buildings via demolition work, is the hardest and heaviest of the common softwoods; exceptionally strong and durable. As it was used for floor joists and beams etc it can come in large dimensions and long lengths, but often contains nails, spikes and bolt holes, so sawmills may be reluctant to machine it. Pitchpine was traditionally used for planking in high-quality yacht construction. Similar to Douglas fir in appearance, but a darker brown colour.

ALASKAN CEDAR - is a particularly fine grained light wood, pale in colour like Sitka spruce, but generally a finer grain. Excellent for planking light canoes and dinghies, and for thwarts etc.

WHITE CEDAR - also popular in North America for planking and general use.

PORT ORFORD CEDAR/LAWSON CYPRESS - as above; strong and durable for its weight, which is between that of cedar and fir. Works and glues well; worth looking for.

WESTERN RED CEDAR - very light but strong for its weight; used for planking canoes, for strip planking, and cold-moulding. Straight grained, easy to work, and very durable. Useful in racing or other ultralight boats, but soft and susceptible to surface damage in exposed places.

SITKA SPRUCE - specifically slow-grown 'aircraft quality': 10 or more growth rings to an inch. (Commercial plantation spruce is junk, but a pile of it may occasionally contain a useful slow-grown piece). Extraordinarily tough and resilient for its light weight; with close straight clear grain it is easy to work. Ideal for spars, oars and light structural work. Not durable. Now very expensive in Britain.

SPRUCE - Norway, Baltic, Northern White - similar to Sitka, generally perhaps not quite as tough but still very good for the same uses.

SCOTS PINE/EUROPEAN 'REDWOOD' - the most common commercial wood in Europe; extremely variable in quality. The best joinery/furniture grade is reasonably strong for its weight, stable, works and glues well.

PINE - many other varieties; good clear stuff is OK for thwarts, bottom boards etc; possibly even spars, with maybe a fractional increase in diameter over spruce or fir.

Tools & Materials

For traditional construction it is generally advisable that boards for planking etc are quarter-sawn, i.e. with the annual growth rings running across the thickness of the board, or diagonally. But with the smaller dimensions we are using in plywood-planked hulls, this is not so relevant, and the more economical, more readily available plain-sawn boards are fine. The only items we are likely to be needing wider boards for are the thwarts, and perhaps a centreboard and rudder.

2-2

It is worth bearing in mind the way that wood is likely to warp in time, with the effects of drying out, especially if this happens too quickly. For example when a wide board that has a fair moisture content, maybe is not completely seasoned, is accustomed to a fairly moist atmosphere around the water then is exposed to hot sunlight. Because of the way in which wood tends to shrink along the lines of the growth rings, a plain-sawn board that comes from some way out from the centre of the log will be inclined to warp as shown in Fig 2-2.

2-3

So if this board is to become a thwart, it may be best to fit it this way up; sunlight on the upper surface may balance out any warping tendency, and if not it is better for the edges to curve down slightly rather than upwards. When preparing edge-glued boards for a transom or centreboard, the curve of the rings should alternate: Fig 2-3.

SEASONING

Green wood contains a lot of moisture, which must be allowed to dry out gradually. If the wood dries too quickly, it will shrink unevenly, and will warp and split. The moisture content, (measured as a percentage of the weight of the wood itself), should be around 12 to 16% for general boatbuilding. But with these lighter 'dry-sailed' boats it can safely err

on the low side, and in an epoxy-sealed hull even less - 8 to 10%.

Wood will generally find its equilibrium in the 12 - 16% range, in conditions of about 'average' temperature and humidity, so it is not a thing to get too anxious about. If the epoxy-building shop is kept to about 66 degrees F - 19C, and fairly dry, the wood should find its equilibrium at somewhere around 8%.

There are two ways of drying timber. Air drying is thought to be best, but takes months or years depending on type and thickness, so is rarely available unless you can do it yourself. So most wood is kiln dried. This method can dry the outside before the inside, and so can be risky if done too fast. But if done carefully it is safe and predictable.

Air dried timber is sticked - that is, thin sticks are placed between the stacked boards, spaced close enough that the boards can not sag. This allows the air to circulate and the moisture content to stabilise gradually. This is worth doing anyway if a quantity of good stuff is to be stored for a long period.

'GREEN' WOOD? (Meaning not unseasoned but ecologically acceptable).

Many boatbuilders, amateur and professional, find themselves so absorbed by the complexities of planning a new boat, and the difficulty of finding the best available materials for the job, that they feel they can not afford to lose too much sleep over worrying about where the wood comes from, and how it is grown - even if it were possible to find out. The average professional boatyard - of necessity an excellent example of pared-to-the-bone economic efficiency - may not feel inclined to go to a lot of trouble to find inferior material for ecological reasons. It's hard enough to find timber of suitable quality. Even though the appalling scale of deforestation that is going on, and the present and potential environmental costs, are well known.

The following considerations are frequently offered as reasons for not being too inhibited about making use of whatever is available.

The building of a boat involves such a relatively minute amount of wood that any hesitation about using a particular exotic species must be a matter of principle, rather than any hope of making a perceptible difference.

In many places the export of timber can be beneficial to the local community, encouraging sustainable management instead of slash-and-burn clearcutting.

An exceptionally fine piece of wood found in the timber yard may as well be used in a beautiful boat, where it will be appreciated for its fine qualities, rather than disappearing into some kitchen to be covered with formica.

On the other hand .... I have seen the clearcutting in Canada, and met with Indian folk from Vancouver Island, who came to Scotland to tell us what was being done to their homeland; I promised those guys I would not be buying new wood from Canada. (A pity - some of it is very good). What the loggers are doing there, as in many other parts of the world, is what has been done to 98-1/2% of the Caledonian forests in Scotland, creating vast areas of virtual desert, where there is practically no life.

Apart from this, I have a strong preference for using local woods as far as possible; I like to work with the trees that grow around here. I love these oaks, pines, elms and ash trees and even the 'foreign' larches.

The Indians reputedly would not cut a tree without showing due respect, asking permission, by means of an appropriate ceremony. I have got as far as scattering handfuls of shavings to the winds at the launching celebration, in gratitude, and promising to plant at least one tree for every piece of wood bought or cut down for a boat (getting a bit behind on this, but I will....). It's all about appreciation and respect for these graceful 'beings' that clothe the earth and enhance our lives in so many ways, and seeing their life as a renewable cycle rather than merely a product to be plundered.

DURABILITY

Some other woods not generally regarded as boatbuilding material can be worth consideration. The usual problem is low durability; however this can be largely alleviated by careful construction, proper ventilation and maintenance, the use of preservatives, and of course epoxy coating. And dry-sailed small craft have much less of a problem, as long as they are not left out in the weather, inadequately covered, for long periods. It is quite depressing how often one sees a good boat left out all winter, partly full of fresh water. That boat is dying, and will be a source of grief and frustration to her owner next summer. 'All that maintenance', he will complain, as he considers a fibreglass replacement .... all he had to do was turn her over, or fit a proper cover.

Birch is rather hard but works well. It does not weather well unless adequately protected. Similar to ash in this respect. Sycamore is used for trim in racing boats.
Sweet chestnut is durable and has been used for planking. Robinia, or black locust, is a medium-weight hardwood, very tough and durable, available in Europe and maybe parts of America. Walnut is good for decorative work. Yew is extraordinarily tough and durable, but rare in anything but small sizes.

PLYWOOD

Marine plywood varies greatly in quality and price. Generally you get what you pay for, and considering all the work you'll be putting into your boat, a few extra pounds/dollars invested in good quality plywood may be well worthwhile.

Bruynzeel, made in Holland, is the best that is commonly available. It is the only brand I have found that can safely be ordered sight-unseen, and consistently comes looking good enough for a top-class bright-finished hull. (But even with Bruynzeel I have had minor faults and surface damage, so it is necessary to check out each sheet carefully before accepting a delivery).

It comes in a wide range of millimetre sizes, which is very convenient for small craft; often you have only a choice between 1/4" and 3/8", and need something in between. There are various types and grades, in either an unusually attractive mahogany, or the lighter occume/gaboon. But Bruynzeel is very expensive.

Equally durable plywood can be obtained for less money - sometimes considerably less. Many varieties are available, unpredictably, from many sources, so all you can do is to shop around and see what you can find. In the cheaper grades of imported plywoods, avoid the kind which has a thick soft inner core, and thin brittle face veneers. Good exterior grade is better, as long as any voids in the core veneers can be found and sealed. Official standards ratings do not seem to count for much; some real junk plywood can somehow conform to all the right standards for marine grade.

Thinner plywoods are made with three veneers. In more expensive 1/4"-6mm ply, and in thicker sizes, expect five; or more than that in over about 3/8"- 10mm. The standard sheet size is 8" x 4"- 1220 x 2440mm, which means that scarph or butt joining is necessary in boats over that length. 10' x 4' or 10' x 5'-3 - 1.22m or 3 x 1.52m sheets are sometimes available.

Some major sources of marine plywood are: In the US - Edensaw (WA) : 1 800 745 3336. Harbor (MD): 1 800 345 1712. In Britain - Silverman: 0181 953 0553. Robbins: 0117 963 3136. Bruynzeel plywood is supplied in the north of England and Scotland by George Hulley: 01389 742 438.

GREEN PLYWOOD?

Unfortunately as plywood is more exclusively made by large international corporations, it becomes more difficult to find out how and where the wood is grown. Although we are using relatively minute quantities, some owners and boatbuilders are beginning to think about it. So I wrote to Bruynzeel in Holland; got a very detailed report on how they own large tracts of land in Gabon, which they are obliged to manage in a sustainable manner, for legal as well as practical reasons. Only a limited number of trees of a given size can be taken out of certtain area in a year; the trees are self-seeding and the system operates on a thirty-year cycle. This is where the material for their gaboon or occume plywood comes from. No mention of the mahogany; so a phone call to Holland was necessary. The best information I could get was that 'as far as we know' their various sources are sustainably managed, but they have no direct control. They expect soon to have an official sustainably-acceptable rating, at least for the gaboon.

In America, marine quality fir plywood is available from Boulter Plywood (MA): 617 666 1340. Robbins intend to make this available in Britain soon.

Finnish Birch plywood is in good supply; it is fairly heavy, has reasonable strength properties, but needs good protection. It is well made and attractive.

Baltic Pine plywood is sometimes available. It is rather light and soft, but has an attractive figure, like fir but lighter and generally more even; good for light boats.

Bruynzeel now offer a useful service: they can put face veneers of any available wood onto a core of their sustainably-grown gaboon plywood. This is usually done with decorative hardwood veneers, but softwoods such as larch, Douglas fir, and pine or spruce may also be available. The cost is not great, and their policy is to supply a single sheet if required, although to order a pack of six is cheaper.

An interesting alternative is larch marine ply; this is made to order in Denmark for a German boatbuilder. Of medium weight, it is tough and strong - it is after all the traditional planking material in Britain and Europe. However it is very expensive: about double the price of mahogany. Ecoboot, Uberwinterungshaven 6, D-21079, Hamburg. Larch plywood is also available from Sommerfield & Thiele, but only in large quantities: 20-plus sheets of each size. Prices are not excessive.

GLUES

EPOXY is now the most popular adhesive, mainly because of its extraordinary versatility. By the use of various fillers, it can be modified for various applications. Is is the most useful and convenient glue for clinker plywood, even though it is expensive, and can be messy to work with. A small percentage of people develop an allergic reaction to it, although some newer brands are supposed to be safer (International Epiglass is "Low odour and free from dangerous phenols"). The use of rubber gloves, and dust masks when sanding, should keep you out of trouble.

Full information and instructions come with the material, so need not be repeated here. What they don't tell you is how to save on the cost: Sanding dust, from the collection bag on an electric sander, works well as a filler; it costs nothing and is the right colour. (Barleycup works in an emergency; it is rather gritty, but a fraction of the price of the proper fillers. It makes a nicer drink than microballoons, though serious coffee drinkers may not agree). Malt vinegar works nearly as well as acetone for cleaning brushes, tools, etc. For cleaning hands, Swarfega (GB) and 3M Paint Buster (NA) work fine. (Get the epoxy before it sets, and wear plastic gloves from now on).

RESORCINOL FORMALDEHYDE

(Cascophen, Weldwood Resorcinol, Aerodux) is an excellent glue, highly durable and relatively easy to work with. It is not a good gap-filling glue - although adding more of the powder hardener helps - so it requires extra care in fitting wood parts together; this can take extra time. Clamping pressure is necessary. Resorcinol tends to leave a dark brown stain, which can be inconvenient with light-coloured wood. Excess can be washed off with water before it sets.

UREA FORMALDEHYDE

(Cascamite, Weldwood Plastic Resin, Aerolite) is also a very good adhesive; cheaper than the others, and easier to use. It comes in liquid form, with fast or slow hardener, but my favourite is the white powder type, with the hardener included; this is simply mixed with water, and is water-washable before it starts to harden. It fills gaps a little better than resorcinol, but nowhere near as well as epoxy. Its creamy colour is virtually invisible when used with spruce, ash etc. Urea is less durable than resorcinol; it retains its strength indefinitely except in conditions of alternate wetting and drying. 'Dry-sailed' racing boats, which are still often built with urea, last indefinitely as long as they are not allowed to get saturated and dried out too often. A boat which is to lie to a mooring and get hauled out for the winter should be built with epoxy or resorcinol. But urea has been used for yacht spars for many years.

Some boatbuilders are experimenting with **POLYURETHANE** glue, which is easy to use. It is a one-part glue needing no mixing; it has a peculiar foaming action which fills gaps, but not structurally. I have yet to hear of anyone brave enough to use it for planking, although builders are getting more adventurous with it. One advantage is that it can be used in high and very low temperatures.

It should be obvious from the above that the advent of epoxy has not actually brought about a great revolution in wooden boatbuilding, as is often claimed. These other glues, although less convenient in some applications, have proved themselves over more than 50 years, so may confidently be used by anyone who is reluctant to work with epoxy for any reason. I mostly work with epoxy, trying to keep as 'clean' as possible, but also use quite a bit of Cascamite where it is appropriate in the small boats. Which is mainly on smaller parts, where there is a close fit without needing much pressure.

All wood-to-wood joints are glued in these boats, so they depend on the gluing being done correctly for their structural integrity. The makers' instructions should be followed carefully. The basic procedure is that the glue is spread evenly on both surfaces,

allowed 10 or 15 minutes to penetrate into the grain of the wood, then the parts are assembled, and sufficient pressure applied with clamps, fastenings etc to squeeze out a little glue all along the joint. This way you know there are no dry places within the joint. You soon learn how much glue is about enough, without the likelihood of a great deal of excess oozing out all over the place.

Wherever possible, lay packaging tape or masking tape along by glued edges; this keeps surplus glue off the surrounding area and saves a lot of time in cleaning up later. This is especially important with epoxy, and in a hull which is to be bright finished.

Excess glue may be wiped off as far as possible with acetone - on epoxy - or water. What's left is easiest removed when it is half set. You won't get it all, because of moulds etc getting in the way, and it is practically impossible to get at all parts of the interior of an inverted hull. But the more you can do as you go along, the easier it will be on the big cleaning-up day.

With epoxy especially the glue and the wood must not be too cold in winter. This can be achieved by means of a polythene sheet draped over the boat, and an electric fan heater used to warm up the relevant parts, and the epoxy. Other glues are less critical, and do not become too thick when cold, but they still like to be
comfortably above freezing.

FINISHES will be dealt with in Chapter 7.

TOOLS

We would need a book to cover this subject properly, but meanwhile a few notes may be useful.

Building a boat can be a far more enjoyable and satisfying experience if suitable high-quality tools are at hand. However for lapstrake plywood construction no special tools are required that are not likely to be found in any reasonably well-equipped home workshop. Although it can be useful to have access to more clamps than you have probably ever seen in one place.

A selection of power tools can save time and effort. But there are few which are likely to justify their cost in the building of one boat, unless they can be put to good use in future projects.

Most timber yards are able to machine wood to order, to whatever sizes are needed. I like if possible to order most of the material for a boat in boards of whatever widths are available, thicknessed to 3/4" or 7/8"- 20 -22mm, and cut strips to size with a circular (table) saw as they are needed. Or shorter or odd-shaped parts with a jigsaw (or bandsaw if available). I find a 'site saw' like builders use is very handy. This is a basic table saw with a pressed-steel top. They are inexpensive, light and portable, yet have powerful motors and usually 12"-300mm tungsten-tipped blades. And they are easy to sell on when the boat is built.

2-4 / 2-5

The following list shows an approximate minimum basic collection of tools - Figs 2-4 and 2-5:

Measuring tape - 6 or 10'-2-3m
12"/300mm steel rule
Try square
Marking gauge
Sliding bevel gauge
Spirit level

Stanley knife
Hand saw - 10 or 12 teeth to an inch
Fine tenon saw
Bow saw or fret saw
Plane - 12 - 14"/300-350mm - No.6
Block plane
3 or 4 chisels - 1/2" to 1-1/4"/12-30mm
Spokeshave
Scraper
Surform or rasp
Files - various
Oilstone
Clamps - 6 plus up to 5" - 125mm
Woodworking vice
Claw hammer
Mallet
Screwdrivers - small, medium, large, preferably including a ratchet
Pliers
Nail punches
Electric drill
Drill bits, countersink bit
Extension lead
Sanding block
Sandpaper - approx. 80 to 400 grit
Putty knife
Dust masks
Hair drier for epoxy

I use a ball-point pen for measuring and marking; it leaves a clean black even line. But pencil marks are more easily erased, so the pencil is kept handy.

2-6 / 2-7 PHASE II TOOL KIT

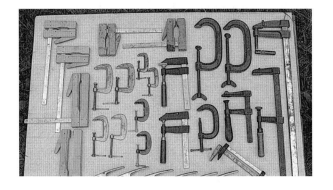

These tools are not essential; a boat can be built without them, although most of them would certainly be useful on occasion if they are available. Some may be necessary for specific jobs on particular boats:

9" /220mm smoothing plane - No.5
2'/600mm roofing square
Rebate plane
Round spokeshave
Plug cutters and drills for 8 and 10gge/
4-5mm screws - drills 5/16-3/8"/8-10mm
Expanding bit
Drawknife
Pincers
Metal-working vice
Stapler (e.g. Arrow T55)

More clamps

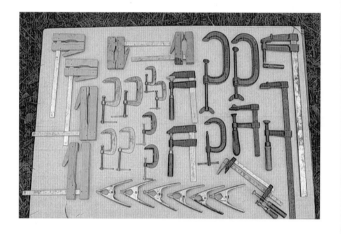

POWER TOOLS

Jigsaw
Variable-speed drill - maybe cordless
Hand planer
Orbital sander
Grinding wheel

Plus - if you have big money to spend and are planning a lot more wood machining:

Bandsaw
Table saw
Planer-thicknesser

2-8 SHARPENING TOOLS

Knowing how to sharpen your plane irons, chisels and spokeshaves properly is so vital to the whole operation that I will give a brief description of how I do it. Blunt tools mean that you will do rough work with a lot more effort; one of life's little pleasures is taking a clean shaving off a piece of wood with a newly-honed blade. The finish is so fine and smooth - and it was so easy!

A new blade comes ground to an angle of about 25 degrees. But it is not ready for use; it must be honed on an oilstone, which means giving it a slightly steeper angle right at the edge. This can then be easily touched up without having to re-grind the original face. Fig 2-8.

2-9

When grinding is necessary, the water-cooled stones are much easier to use; the usual high-speed dry grinding wheel is difficult because it quickly burns the temper out of the steel, turning it blue right at the edge. It is then soft and brittle. These stones are also generally much too narrow for a plane iron.

2-10

A few drops of oil are put on the oil-stone. The bevelled edge of the blade is laid flat on the stone, then raised a wee bit - about 2 or 3 degrees: Fig 2-10. Then it is worked steadily back and forth with a moderate even pressure. Just a few strokes will do it, with a new or newly-ground blade.

2-11

Then the blade is turned over and laid flat on the stone, and lightly pushed back and forth a couple of times to remove the burr.

The final stage is to strop the edge by drawing it back a few times each side on a piece of leather - Fig 2-11.

2-12

When the blade has been honed many times the honing angle may be increased, or you may want to just touch up the edge a little before re-grinding. As before, lay the ground edge on the stone, then begin raising the blade very gradually, while moving it forward and back. As you get to the right angle, i.e. when it is beginning to cut the very tip of the edge, you will feel a little more resistance as the stone begins to cut the edge. You may even be able to hear a slightly harder grinding sound.

Don't go any higher than this, or you will be cutting too steep an angle, and hastening the day when re-grinding will be necessary. Having found the right angle, I try to back off the tiniest amount, then a few strokes at this backed-off angle will take it back to the edge. This way you keep the bevel at or near the original minimal honing angle; it is too easy to make it a little steeper each time, and finish up with a not very sharp tool.

In theory, a blade used for softwood can be ground at a sharper angle: about 20 degrees and for hardwood up to 30 degrees. But in practice it is necessary to compromise, if working both soft and hard woods. 25 degrees works well.

(Don't be too impressed with talk of 'razor-sharp' tools; a chisel ground as sharp as a razor would barely begin to cut anything harder than balsa wood before shattering its edge).

A plane's backing iron is set up to 1/16" - 1 to 1.5mm back from the edge of the blade. This works well for rough work, taking off coarse shavings where there is no need to worry about the finish. But it will tear up an area of grain which comes out the wrong way: Fig 2-12.

2-13

When going for a fine finish, especially on a piece which has a wavy grain, the backing iron can be set very close to the edge. This turns the shaving back immediately, and will not tear up a bit of misdirected grain. Fig 2-13 shows a backing iron set close to the edge of the blade for fine work, and another set coarse for a deeper cut.

SAFETY EQUIPMENT

Professional woodworking shops have to conform to all sorts of safety regulations. I don't believe they make any difference. Anyone intelligent enough to handle woodworking tools can soon enough see they can cut soft flesh as easily as wood. In theory the unregulated home builders should be more vulnerable, but in fact they rarely, if ever, seem to cause themselves any permanent damage. It's like sailing a boat: no amount of officially prescribed safety gear or EU Directives will compensate for a lack of innate seamanship: common sense, skill and experience.

Two things are worth bearing in mind: sharp tools are safer than blunt ones, as they cut with less effort, and are therefore more easily controlled. And most accidents happen when the operator is tired or in a stressed-out state.

Common sense also indicates not breathing in lots of dust and solvents. Simple

dust masks work quite well; the type with a one-way valve work better. Most effective are the larger ones with replaceable filters, with various filters available for certain vapours. But these are comparatively inconvenient and uncomfortable, so are more likely to be kept for use with synthetic finishes, or sanding epoxy, or anytime you are feeling sensitive to whatever is in the air. A dust mask should be worn for some time after a sawing or sanding job, as the dust hangs in the air for quite a long time. Good ventilation helps a lot; it is difficult to achieve in winter when keeping warm is a priority, but it is essential when painting or varnishing.

Gloves are also necessary to keep glue etc off your hands, when involved in sizeable gluing operations. The thin plastic free ones you sometimes get at garages might last for one or two small jobs; latex rubber 'medical examination' gloves are quite tough; a whole box will last for at least one boat.

FASTENINGS

Very few fastenings are needed in these hulls. Planks are normally fastened only at the ends, the glue being sufficient along the lands. However a builder of a larger seagoing vessel, planked in 1/2"-12mm or heavier plywood, may like to screw the planks together, so he is not depending entirely on the adhesion of the surface veneers, but has the whole thickness of the ply held down to the next plank. Some boatbuilders however think this is quite unnecessary. But small craft hulls, without plank fastenings, stay together even beyond the stage when they need new frames, transoms, decks. A few fastenings will not save a bad glue joint.

I have been using fewer fastenings in each boat; ultimately the Acorn 13 we built recently has no permanent fastenings in her hull at all - only the few removeable ones needed for sternsheets and bottom boards.

Bronze woodscrews and Gripfast nails are used almost universally. Visible screws may be counterbored and plugged, in 'yacht-finished' boats. Nails may be punched and filled with an epoxy/sawdust mix.

A number of temporary screws will be used; these of course may be steel. A wipe with soft soap prevents them getting glued permanently into the hull. A stapler can be useful for light plywood and other small parts. Get a good powerful one.

Tools & Materials

HOW GOOD DOES IT HAVE TO BE?

The roughest boat ever built to one of my designs was a flat-bottom Seahorse Skiff built by my friend James. He was experiencing a time of drastic changes in his life; building and sailing this boat helped him to work through it.

The construction work was basic carpentry - to put it politely. James sailed her all around the Thames Estuary for 3 months before he got around to giving the hull a couple of coats of oil; he stuck matches in odd nail holes to keep the water out of her. The boat lived out in the weather for years, including 6 months neglected on a beach in Spain. After 7 or 8 years we ripped most of the remaining face veneer off the bottom and sides with a belt sander; slapped some paint on her at last, and she was good for another few seasons.

This demonstrates that a boat roughly built of cheap plywood, not finished properly, and not maintained at all, will still last longer than a fibreglass one.

But the point of the story is this: fine joinery and a fancy finish are not essential, as long as the structure is basically sound. James's boat has been a great success, and has served her purpose well. He was totally unconcerned about how she might look in comparison with some of the 12-coats-of-varnish fancy toys at the Wooden Boat Show.

2-14

Here is a less extreme but more typical example - Fig 2-14: The builder of this Mouse Pram in Ireland thought about how much work it would be to plane this transom flat, with its badly-butted joints: quite a bit. How necessary it was structurally: not at all. And how satisfying it would be to have it smooth and flat: not very. He confessed that he was "...not the world's greatest carpenter, but epoxy is wonderful stuff". Obviously the crew are quite content with their wee ship.

By all means build the finest boat you can, making use of the opportunity to practice and refine your skills. More than one builder has written to me and said it's the most satisfying thing he's ever done; so it seems good to make the most of the opportunity to create something beautiful. This is after all one of the major reasons for building wooden boats. I just hope prospective builders will not be put off by thinking they are not clever enough, or that they have to conform to some standard of craftsmanship.

LINING OFF

3-1

The layout of the planks is the most important aspect of the appearance of a lapstrake boat, apart from the basic shape of the hull. If the planking is lined off well, it looks very fine; if not, it can ruin the appearance of the boat.

If you are not working to a stock plan with handy marks on the mould patterns to indicate where the planks go, the following system will enable you to do a professional looking job. But unlike boatbuilders' methods, which are done on the moulds after they are set up, this one is worked out on paper. No written method can take account of all the many variations in hull shapes, so it will all be checked out by eye before any planking material is cut. This system will give the builder a place to start from, with the flexibility to allow for the requirements of any particular hull. The final result should be a planking pattern that gives a fair and natural progression from the midsection into the ends, with each strake tapering evenly and proportioned properly in relation to the others. Fig 3-1.

The first thing to decide is how many strakes there will be on each side. Generally the number found in a traditional hull may be reduced by at least two. But although even fewer strakes than that may be sufficient structurally, if they become too wide the boat may begin to lose something of her traditional appearance. Also the greater angle from one strake to the next may create a problem with the widths of the lands.

The next question is the proportional width of each strake. The garboard and the next strake or two are the widest; the narrowest are those around the turn of the bilge, and the topsides.

Topside strakes may be around 75% of the width of the garboards. Variable according to hull form: in a high deadrise hull with slack bilges, the strakes can be more even in width: about 80 or 85%. With a broad bottom and firm bilges, the topside strakes will need to be narrower in proportion to the garboards - about 66%.

The next strake outboard from the garboard strake, the 'broadstrake', is the same width as the garboard, at the midsection. Then there will be one or two of intermediate width before the narrower bilge strakes are reached.

The sheer strake and garboard are the first ones to think about. The sheerstrake is the most important visually; the garboard, although the least visible, provides an important foundation for the lining off pattern.

The sheerstrake in finer-lined skiffs and canoes is usually shaped to the same proportions, fore and aft, as the strakes below it. In more substantial craft it may be slightly deeper amidships, and tapered less towards the ends. Somewhere between a line parallel to the sheer and a fully tapered plank. If in doubt the latter scheme is generally safe.

The depth of the gunwale rubbing strake (sheerguard) is added to the depth of the sheerstrake.

SHAPES AND PROPORTIONS

3-2

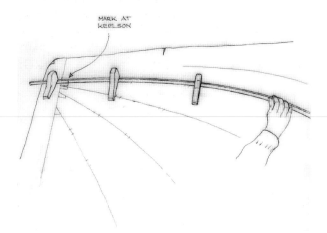

It is most convenient to work with paper patterns of the moulds, and a lines plan. But the lofted lines will work - with a bit more wear on the knees. The first thing needed is the girth at the midsection, from the outer edge of the keelson to the underside of the gunwale rubbing strake. (The 'midsection' is usually at the first station abaft a point halfway along the hull - in any case the one with the greatest girth). A light batten is bent around the midsection mould shape, ideally with weights - Fig 3-2. Millimetres are convenient to work with (I am not recommending metric conversion).

3-3

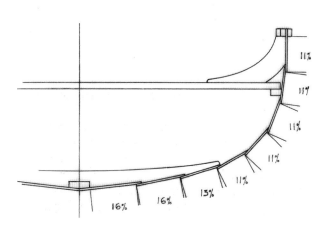

Using the Guillemot dinghy as an example: the midsection girth is 925mm. A table is now worked out which gives a percentage of the midsection for each strake. Assuming 8 strakes a side - topside strakes 70% of garboard, it works out as shown in Fig 3-3.

It takes a little juggling with the percentages to get them to add up. (Or a cleverer mathematician than me). Here we are one fat mm out, which is quite close enough at this stage.

The following examples show contrasting hull shapes, and how they are proportioned by the same method.

3-4

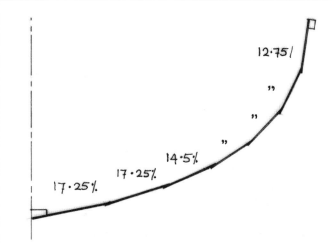

Fig 3-4: Acorn Skiff - light hull, slack bilge, 7 strakes. Topsides 74% of garboard width.

3-5

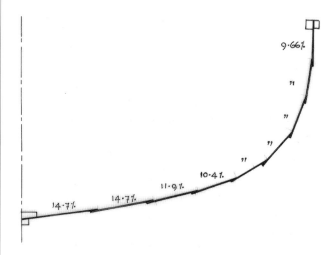

Fig 3-5: Fulmar - larger dayboat, broad bottom, firmer bilge. 9 strakes. Topsides 66% of garboard.

THE SHEERSTRAKE

3-6

A

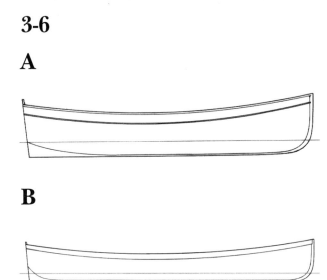

B

If the sheerstrake is to be the same width, towards the ends, as the strakes below it, ignore the next four paragraphs. If wider, it is now drawn in profile on the lines plan. Add 1/4" to 1/2" -5-10mm - to the topside strake width, and mark this dimension at one station aft and two forward of the 'midships mould.

A point about 75 to 80% of the 'midships width is marked on the stem. Aft, the taper may be about the same. But, if the boat has a broad deep transom - Fig 3-6a - the after part of the sheerstrake may be wider: perhaps 85 - 90%. In a longer leaner hull 3-6b - the sheerstrake may taper more sharply aft, to about 60 or 70%.

The sheerstrake may be virtually parallel to the sheer for a short distance amidships, gradually beginning to taper off. The aim is for a fair line, bearing a close relationship to the sheer all along its length. At any point forward and aft it should not appear too parallel, nor too sharply tapered.

Now leave the wide sheerstrake and proceed as if lining off a hull with one less strake. From here on 'sheer' means the lower edge of the sheerstrake. You'll need to calculate a new set of girth percentages (the previous example got 4 strakes below the sheer at 12.1%, one at 15%, and the broad and garboard at 18.3%).

THE GARBOARD STRAKE

The garboard will provisionally be be same percentage of the girth at each station. This can be calculated on the mould patterns, then the dimensions scaled down and marked on the lines plan sections. Then the half-breadths and heights of these points are transferred to the plan and profile.

3-7

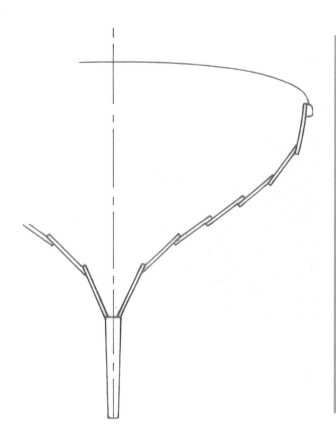

With a broad transom the proportion may remain the same aft to the transom. But with a small wineglass transom with a strong tuck (reverse turn) it can be a little narrower, to avoid a sharp upward twist and maintain some extra width in the hood ends of the other strakes, which will become quite narrow on the smaller girth of this type of transom - Fig 3-7.

In the forebody it is advisable to reduce the width of the garboard as far as it will comfortably go, so as to reduce any tendency for the strakes above it to get squeezed into narrower shapes towards the bow, as the girth

Lining Off

diminishes rapidly forward of amidships. If they taper too sharply they may ultimately appear to droop toward the stem.

3-8

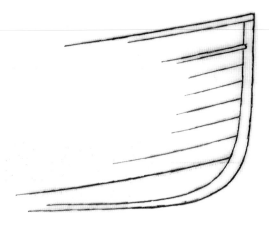

TRAD. PULLING BOAT

SAILING DINGHY

At the stem, the garboard will sweep up to near the waterline, or a little above it. With a straight keel and deep forefoot, it will be wide forward. But if there is a lot of rocker and a cutaway forefoot, it will appear quite narrow - Fig 3-8.

What we want is a line that looks fair in profile, plan, and the body plan (sections). The profile is the important one, but the others will help to achieve a fair line.

In plan (looking down), the garboard may appear to twist in sharply to the stem, and looking aft at the sections it may even sag down; this is normal and is OK as long as we have a good sweep up in profile.

3-9

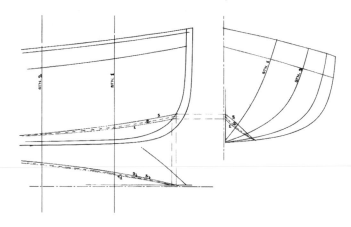

Fig 3-9 illustrates the development of the Guillemot's garboard, to show how it may be pushed around when it does not happen to come out right first time - which it probably won't.

Line 1 was nice and low down, but maybe a little too low at the stem. And in the body plan a sharp upward turn. No. 2 may be better; let's take that further, try to get up to the waterline, and see what happens. No 3 then is getting rather wide across Stns 1 and 2; not much of a sweep up to the stem in profile, and a bit of a twist inwards in plan. No. 2 seems a good compromise; it is a fair and easy line in all three views.

THE GRAPH

3-10

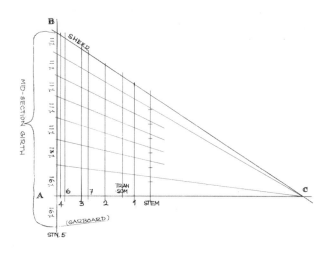

To find the proportions of the rest of the planks, a graph is used, like that in Fig 3-10. The line AB represents the girth at the midsection, minus the garboard. Minus also the wider sheerstrake, if that is relevant. (In this case 'sheer' now refers to the underside of the sheerstrake).

A vanishing point is marked some distance from point A; as far as convenient - on your table rather than somewhere out the window. Within reach of a 3 or 4' - 1m+ straight edge.

From point B, the midsection girth, take a line to the vanishing point, C. Then mark the girth of each station on BC, by moving the measuring tape along AC, perpendicular to AC, until the girth dimension in question meets BC.

Now the plank width percentages at the midsection that we decided on are marked on AB. By taking a line from each percentage mark to the vanishing point C, the point where each one crosses the girth lines gives the width of the strake at each station.

This is the theory; unfortunately things may be different in practice. Towards the stern it works; forward of the midsection, it may be OK in a longer hull, but usually it will be necessary to even up the widths towards the stem to some extent, so the topside strakes will not taper too sharply. This is especially so if there is a wide proportional difference between upper and lower strakes.

In any case, we need a further girth line forward, representing the stem. With a straight stem it's easy; extend the garboard, in profile, to the forward perpendicular, or a vertical extension of the stem. With a raked stem, take a line from the top of the stem to the point where the garboard meets the stem. Or if the stem is strongly raked, draw up a new station line from this point, and measure its girth. Either way, this becomes the foremost girth line on the graph.

3-11

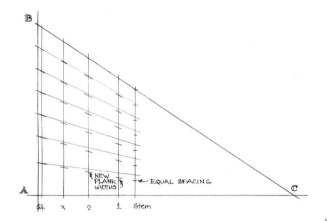

Now divide up this line equally by the number of strakes - Fig 3-11. Take the width lines from AB to these equal divisions, instead of to C. This gives us even spacing of the planks forward.

I find this works well in the beamy type of hull with wide variation in the mid-section widths.

3-12

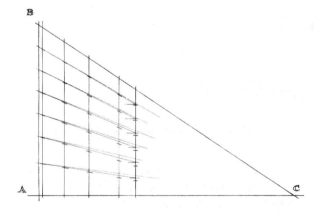

But with the longer hull with more even percentages, a compromise can be advisable. Thinking that the strakes do not necessarily have to be quite equal forward, I sometimes work to a mark half way between the C line and the even-spacing mark: Fig 3-12. The Acorn Skiff was done this way - Fig 3-13 (over).

3-13

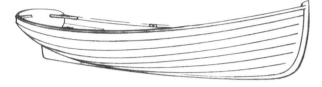

3-14

On the beamier Guillemot, however, using the half-way method, those lower strakes still came out rather wide, like Fig 3-14.

3-15

The final lines were achieved by going back not quite to the even marks, but about half way towards them: Fig 3-15.

Here it is apparent that the 2 or 3 strakes above the garboard can appear to be getting wider forward, owing to the twist in them as they move aft. But the upper 3 or 4 must be gently tapering forward; they must not be allowed to sag down as the approach the stem. This applies especially to the sheerstrake.

The boat shown is the prototype 'Ptarmigan'; the garboard is rather low, and the next strake a bit wide. The topside strakes appear slightly narrow at the stem, still on the lean side in proportion to the lower strakes. It's not bad! - I'm being extra critical.

3-16

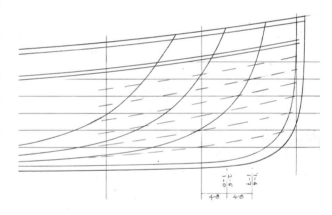

Fig 3-16 shows the final design, which has gone a little further in the direction of even spacing. See also Fig 3- 1.

In a double-ended hull of course all the above remarks referring to the bow will apply to the stern also.

Unfortunately we can not see exactly how the layout we now have is going to look, until it is all dimensioned out on the patterns, and transferred to the lines plan.

But now we have the widths of all the strakes at every station, these can be transferred to the mould patterns, or the body plan, using a compass or dividers. There will be some trial and error to get them to add up; because we are working with short straight lines around the curved mould shape, we need to err a fraction under on each one.

Now at last it is possible to check the whole thing out, by measuring the height of each mark at each station, above and below the waterline (or from a base line).

It is not essential to record every one; I usually take two strakes down from the sheer right through, and all of them across the first 3 or 4 stations, to see how they line up in the more critical, and less predictable, bow area. The heights are marked lightly in pencil, and drawn through with a batten.

The infinite possible variations make it impossible for this or any other method to give totally predictable results, so some adjustments may be necessary. The strakes should still be getting narrower as they approach the stem; curving gently upwards, without getting too bunched up. Four or five topside strakes will come out even at the stem, then 2 or 3 approaching the garboard will be getting slightly wider.

If it still doesn't look right, it may be necessary to go back and reconsider the even-spacing question on the graph. Possibly moving towards or away from evenly space divisions, to vary the lines as they approach the bow.

It occasionally happens that after all this the topside strakes still taper too quickly from amidships, and will need to be eased down a little lower at around 1/3 to 1/4 of the hull length. This is because the girth here is sharply reduced from the midsection girth, while the freeboard is increasing.

In the last resort, if there is any lingering doubt, the lines may be checked on the moulds after they are set up. Light battens are tacked to each mould at the land marks, to show exactly how the lining-off will look. Lengths of string with drawing pins will give quite a good impression (though a slightly bumpy one).

In the end, the only rule is to get it looking good. The problem with this, as John Gardner points out, is that it depends who is doing the looking, and, to carry this a step further, how much looking they have done. If you look at enough boats, photos of boats, and drawings of boats, you will soon develop a fair idea of what looks right for the hull type you have in mind

3-17 THE LANDS

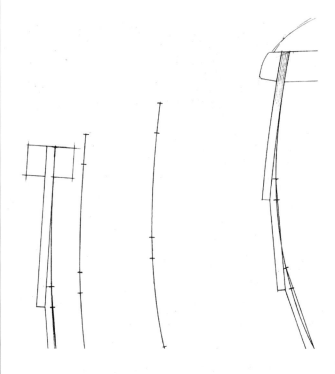

Finally the widths of the lands are marked on the mould patterns. The laps are usually about 5/8" - 15mm with 1/4"- 6mm plywood, or 3/4"- 20mm with 3/8"- 8-10mm ply. The marks that we have achieved after all this work represent the lower, visible edge of each strake, so the land marks will go above them. Fig 3-17 shows the original lining-off marks, the higher land marks, and how the planks will be fitted in relation to them.

Lining Off

SETTING UP

The **BUILDING PROCEDURE** is based on the round-bilge hull type, with about 8 strakes to a side. Builders of other types should look out for extra or optional notes, signified by the following symbols: *P* refers to prams. *DE* refers to the double-enders. *D* means dories. (Either of these could also apply in some cases to a dory skiff or other 'wide-strake' hull).

ABBREVIATIONS:

CL means centreline.

BF means the top edge of the building frame.

FSP refers to the full size mould and/or stem patterns.

'Upper' means towards the sheer - even when the hull is upside down.

4-1

Before you get started, you might need to take a few measurements, just to make sure .... it has happened!

4-2

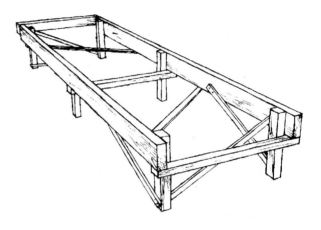

The **BUILDING FRAME** consists of two bearers of about 1-1/2" x 3" - 40 x 75mm for small craft; up to 2 x 4" or 2 x 6" - 50 x100 or150mm for larger boats. Bigger is better. The small boat's bearers may rest on trestles or a long table; otherwise legs and braces are fitted about as shown.

The Construction Plan should show necessary dimensions, and the positions of the end beams. The height may be increased or reduced a couple of inches if the builder is tall or short. For longer hulls it is usual to use shorter pieces bolted together to make up the bearers.

4-3

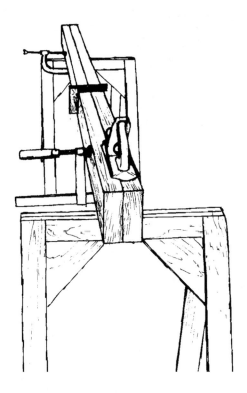

4-4

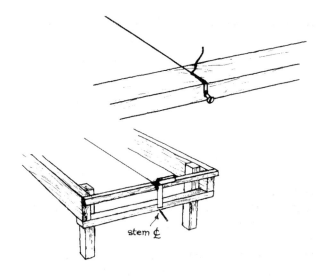

stem ℄

A string **CENTRELINE** is set up at the level of the top of the frame (hereafter referred to as BF height).

4-5

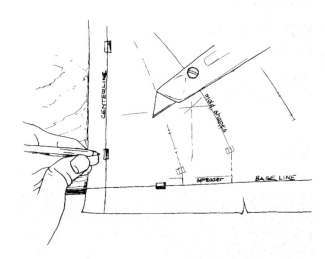

The top edges are planed straight and square, using a straight edge, string line etc. The bearers may be clamped together for planing, then laid flat, edge to edge, to check the high points.

When straight, clamp them together again and mark the stations, squared across the top edges, to dimensions on the Lines and Construction plans.

Assemble with screws or bolts; fit diagonal braces for rigidity. Level the frame up both ways with a spirit level. Fasten the legs to the floor if possible. (At times when it was not easy, e.g. on a concrete floor, I have marked the positions of the legs on the floor, and shoved the frame back into place whenever it started to wander around).

MOULDS are made up from 1/2" -10-12mm plywood. Shuttering ply or Sterling Board ('Oriented Strand Board') are OK if flat; (they are often not stored flat, but minor twists can be straightened out later with battens tacked to the moulds).

Chipboard and MDF (fibreboard) can also be used, though they are a little harder to cut.

Some smaller moulds can be got partly out of the middle of larger ones to save material.

The edge of the plywood sheet - or a straight line - is set exactly under the BF or Base Line on the mould patterns. A spike, scriber or compass point is used to mark the Centreline

Setting Up

(CL), plank lands, keelson, waterline etc. Some small 'windows' are cut out of the pattern, on CL and BF lines. These lines can then be marked on the back of the paper, so the pattern, when turned over, can be lined up for marking the other side of the mould, using the same holes made by the spike.

The marks showing the mould shape are joined up using a thin flexible batten, on a round-bilge hull, or a steel rule, for prams, double-enders and dories - the 'wide-strake' hulls.

Make sure you have all relevant reference lines and marks clearly visible on port and starboard sides.

Cut the mould out with a jigsaw - or whatever (a bandsaw is ideal) - either right on the line, if your saw can cut clean and straight, or just outside of it, and trim back to the line with a block plane. Cut out the notch for the keelson or hog.

4-6

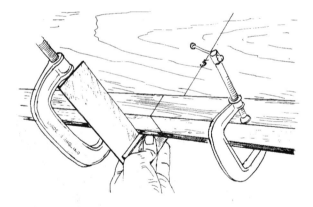

SPREADERS or **SPALLS** ideally should be dead straight. A slight bend may be corrected by lining it up along the edge of the mould. If the mould is narrower than the building frame, the spreader should extend two or three inches outboard of the BF bearers, to help in lining it up with the others.

The spreader is glued flush with the BF edge of each mould. (Or screwed to make recycling easier - clamp in place then screw). CL is marked right round the spreader.

4-7

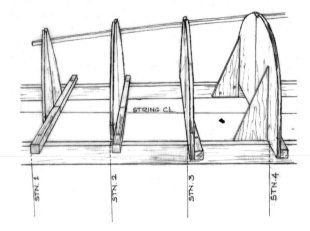

SPREADERS, with moulds, are screwed to the building frame, on the 'inside' of the Station lines - i.e. aft of the Station, forward of amidships, and forward of the Station towards the stern. All must line up on the CL.

Use 8 or 10g - 4-5mm screws. (Shorter screws may be counterbored into the spreader - but not too deep and tight or they can be awful hard to get out later).

4-8

Two moulds, one forward and one aft, are braced up vertically, using struts or plywood brackets.

(If the moulds are made from 3/4" - 20mm material, all may be set up with brackets like these, and the spreaders dispensed with).

4-9

Light battens are then tacked to each mould, each side, to hold them upright, and equidistant top and bottom from each other mould. Any slight twist in a mould can thus be corrected. (See also Figs 4-15 and 59).

4-10

Sight up all the spreaders from each end to see they are in line; this can be done with straight edge(s) clamped to the end mould(s). Any that are low can be shimmed up; ones that are too high should be removed and cut away a little underneath. Vertical straight sticks clamped to the moulds amidships help to line them up on CL.

4-11

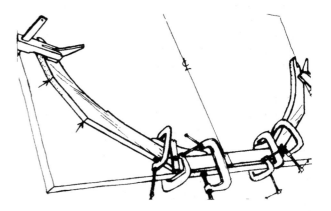

D **DORY FRAMES** - parts are cut out and cleaned up; notches for gunwales and limber holes are cut out before assembly.

Knees may be cut slightly thick to be planed flush later. They are screwed (and plugged if necessary) after gluing.

The plan is positioned so that parts can be clamped to the bench over it, with plastic sheet over the plan to prevent the glue sticking to it.

4-12

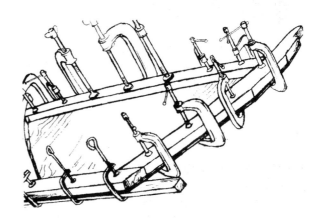

D **BULKHEADS,** if any, are glued with clamps or copper nails.

4-13

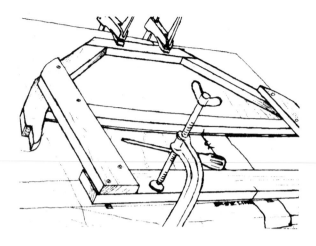

D uprights are screwed to frames and spreaders.

4-14

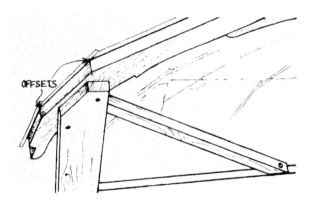

D **BRACES** are fitted. Offset points are checked and clearly marked.

4-15

D moulds and frames are set up.

4-16

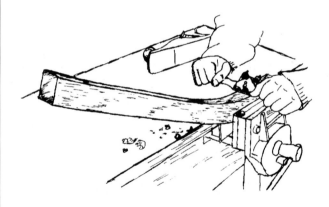

STEM pieces are cut and joined about as shown on the plan. The position of joints is not critical; may depend on the size of stock. Clean up the inner edges. The pieces may be left well oversize, then cut to shape from the pattern after assembly.

4-17

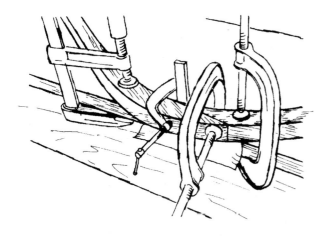

Check the fit over the pattern; glue flat on the bench.

Clean up sides as necessary. Mark CL all round inside and out. Clearly mark all relevant lines: forward perpendicular, sheer, DWL, Station 1, and especially the plank lands.

4-18

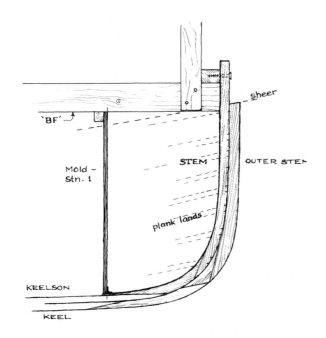

This built-up stem construction is, in theory, not as strong as a laminated stem; however when it is all assembled it is very solid, and certainly more substantial than is structurally necessary.

4-19

A 'halved' joint: another way to assemble a built-up stem from thinner boards. The parts are glued before the stem is cut to shape with bandsaw or jigsaw.

But some builders like to use a laminated stem, and it certainly looks fine, especially in the lighter fine-lined skiffs and canoes.

4-20

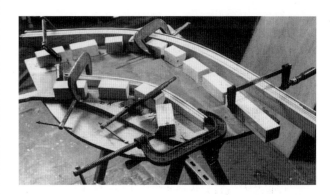

LAMINATED STEM. The inside curve of the inner stem is marked on the bench or on a suitable piece of stout plywood. The ends are brought in about 1/8" - 4mm to make a tighter curve, which should be enough to counteract the tendency to straighten out. Wood blocks are firmly screwed to the bench inside this shape.

The laminations are about 1/8 to 5/32" - 3-4mm. They may be reluctant to take up the required curve; in any case there will be quite a bit of pressure required to bring them all in to the blocks. They may be brought in gradually, an inch or two at a time, taking up a little on the clamps several time over a day or two. Here a knee is being prepared also.

4-21

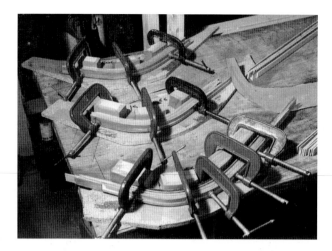

If your boat needs laminated knees they can be done now while you are in a laminating frame of mind.

When the laminations are fitting to the blocks, have a look to see where extra clamps may be needed between the blocks.

4-22

Plastic sheet or packaging tape is applied to the bench; glue is applied to both faces of each lamination - except the outside - and the whole mess is assembled. Apply pressure to the clamps a little at a time, working from the middle of the curve towards the ends. Do not apply full pressure at first; get them close, then see if all the laminations are flush at the top. If necessary tap them down with a hammer and a block of wood. Then take up on the clamps, still working from the centre outwards, with enough pressure to get the glue squeezing out all along, but don't overdo it.

4-23

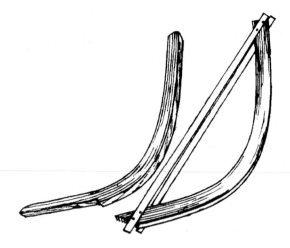

The **OUTER STEM** is laminated around the inner stem in the same way.

Light battens are tacked to it to hold it in shape.

4-24

The stem (and knees) are planed flat and cleaned up all round.

4-25

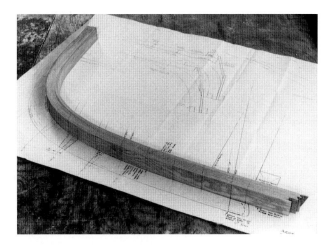

The stem is laid on the plan, and all relevant points marked; note the plank land positions here.

4-26

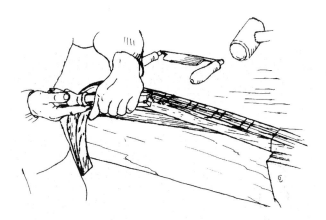

The stem may be roughly bevelled, so there will be less to be taken off after it is set up. If there is no inner bevel line - bearding line - on the plan or the lofted lines, cut it back to about 45 degrees, working down to the forward line, leaving the flat forward face at its specified width. Start with sawcuts at 45 degrees, about 3" -75mm apart, which make it easier to remove the bulk of the wood with a chisel.

4-27

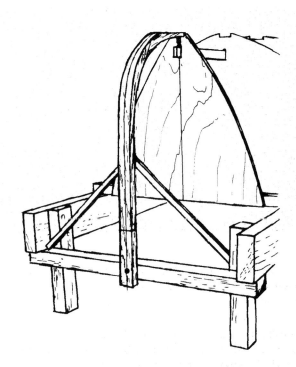

The stem is accurately fitted to the forward BF beam, and to the first mould.

Double-check all relevant dimensions from the Construction and Lines plans, especially sheer height and forward perpendicular, in relation to BF.

Check that the stem is vertical with a spirit level, etc; line it up fore and aft by sighting along the keel line from each end.

Screw it to the forward beam. Fit it to the first mould with an angle bracket or wood block.

Add braces to support the stem against side pressure (which will be considerable at times when you're planking up).

Setting Up

4-28

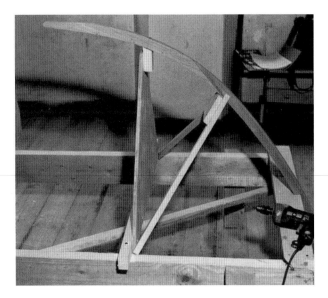

DE The raked stem is notched into the BF beam. The sternpost is prepared and fitted in the same way.

4-29

D The dory stem is in one piece, screwed to BF beam and the first mould.

4-30

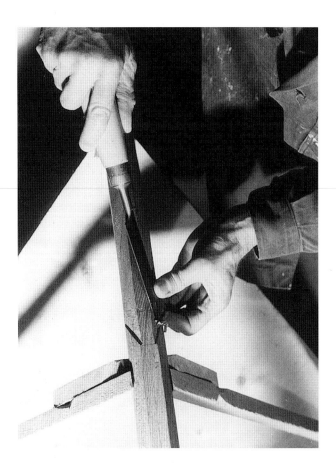

*DE*D* Note that if the garboards will be thicker than the topside strakes, the difference in thickness is taken off at the forward face (to be fully faired later) so that the outer faces of the planking will finish up flush, and the outer stem will be the same width all round. E.g. if the garboard is 3mm thicker than the sides, then 1/8" - 3mm is taken off each side; if the flat face of the stem is 3/4" - 20mm, it is reduced to 1/2" - 14mm in way of the garboards. See also Fig 4-51.

4-31

TRANSOM boards are planed straight and square on the edges, and glued together. Sash cramps are useful, but blocks and wedges work fine.

4-32

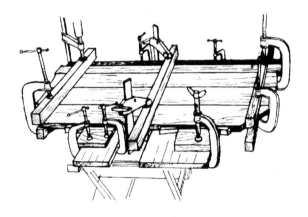

A more complex setup used for a larger transom, where the boards were slightly bent, and needed to be held flat together. The wedges tighten the boards against the beam clamped at the back.

4-33

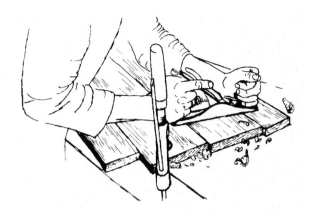

The faces are smoothed up with a fine set plane, across and then along the grain.

4-34

TRANSOM MOUNTING POSTS are set up on the building frame, using the angle and other relevant dimensions from the plans. Clamp in place, check everything and screw. Mark the sheer height.

Note the angle brackets for fixing the transom; these go on the inside so they'll be easier to remove. The screw holes can usually be placed so as to be out of sight under quarter knees, sternsheets etc. If not, they will be filled later with colour-matched filler.

Setting Up

4-35

A **PLYWOOD TRANSOM** is an option; it saves a little weight. The ply is usually the same as the planking stock. It is cut to shape and the framing pieces glued to it.

The transom is marked up from the patterns and cut out. (In my designs the transom is drawn to its inside face, and faired down later. So the aft face will be smaller, finding its own shape when faired down for the planking).

4-36

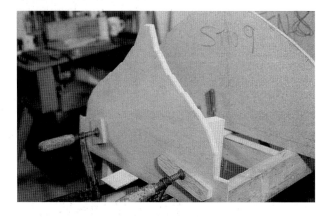

The top of the transom may be left straight; if there is enough wood, it may extend to the BF, which facilitates setting it up. Also the straight top gives a handy reference line when the hull is turned over, and helps in aligning it when fitting thwarts etc, Its final shape is marked before the transom is set up.

The CL is marked on forward and aft faces. Sheer height is marked across the inner face.

4-37

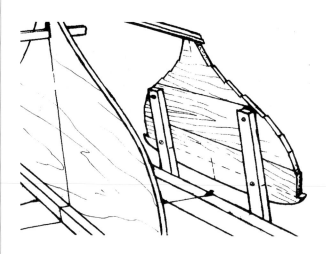

Acorn 15-Mole-Badger With a narrower transom, the posts must go inboard of the BF bearers, so are screwed to the aft beam, which is bevelled or notched to the correct angle.

4-38

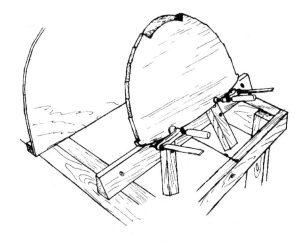

P The same method is used for the small bow transom on the prams. (This bow is partly bevelled for the bow planking).

4-39

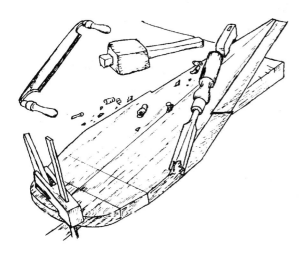

D A dory transom has some interesting changing bevels; lofting it fully is complicated. If working to the outside shape, leave plenty to spare all round - again working to the inside shape is easier. The John Dory and Amberjack plans show forward and aft faces. The latter is still slightly oversize, leaving a little stock to be faired off later, as with a normal transom.

The step shown is equal to the thickness of the garboards; the second strake will sit outside the garboard here.

4-40

The **KEELSON or HOG** is cut a few inches over length. It will be notched into, or scarphed to the stem forward (*DE* and aft). A centreline is marked top and bottom. The taper is cut in the forward part of the keelson.

4-41

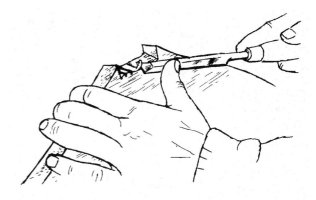

The transom notch is bevelled, working to sawcuts which are made in line with a batten laid over the last two moulds. A transom with a tuck in it is too narrow for a notch - see Fig 4-37.

The keelson is positioned in the transom and mould notches, held down at each end, and each station is clearly marked on top (underneath!).

It may be roughly bevelled, to within 1/16" - 2mm of the angles shown on the mould patterns. It is easier to remove the bulk of the wood on the bench.

If the keel line is curved up strongly aft, the keelson may be split aft with a bandsaw (preferably) so it will bend more easily. Or the whole keelson can be made from two laminations.

4-42

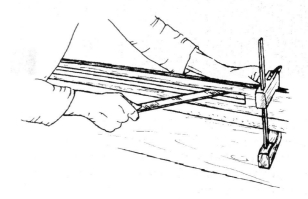

The centreboard case slot is cut, ideally with a router, circular saw, or jigsaw. If the latter it will need to be cleaned up carefully so the edges are straight.

4-43

The keelson is first glued and clamped to the stem.

4-44

This keelson is laminated from two parts. Note the Spanish windlass. A brace to the roof may serve the same purpose, which is to ensure that the keelson is in contact with all the moulds.

4-45

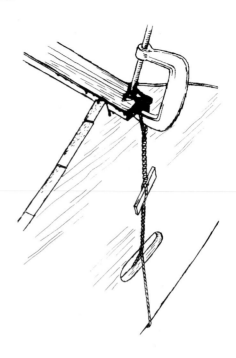

The after end is held down with a Spanish windlass. Note the step for the clamp.

4-46

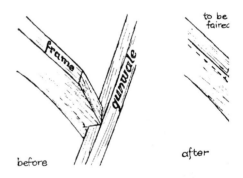

D GUNWALES are usually fitted after the hull is turned over, but not on the dories. They are notched into the frames ....

4-47

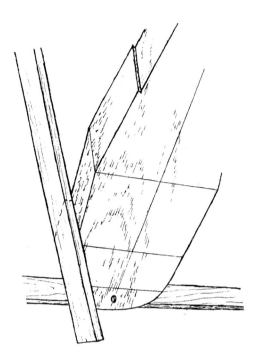

D and the transom. Or they can butt up against the inside face of the transom. This is a little harder to do; may look better as you won't see the end of the gunwale; it is not as strong, but strong enough once everything is glued together. If cutting notches, fit the forward end first.

4-48

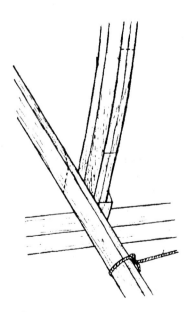

D The gunwale is clamped or tied to the frames, and bent in towards the stem. Mark the angle ....

4-49

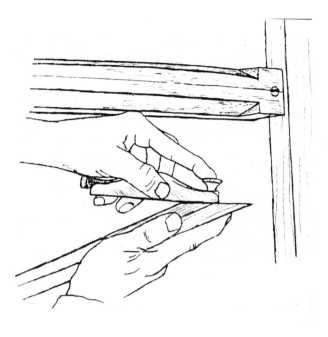

D and cut about 1/16" - 2mm over length. Trim with a block plane.

4-50

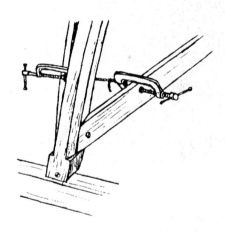

D Clamps and ropes are used to hold both gunwales in to the stem, while they are screwed down. (The clamps may also be hauled down if necessary to twist the gunwales in line with the stem). Use minimal tension, so as not to straighten the gunwales; ideally the tension is eased a little before the screw is tightened home.

Setting Up

4-51

FAIRING for the planking requires care and patience. The setup will not look much different after you've finished, but a properly faired hull is essential for good plank lines and a fair sheerline.

4-52

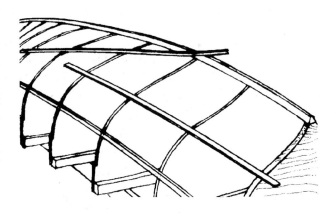

Keelson, stem, transom and moulds are faired with planes and spokeshaves, using a hardwood batten of about 3/8" x 1/2" - 10 x 12mm or larger, maybe tapered towards one end. The batten is laid fore and aft and diagonally all over the hull.

4-53

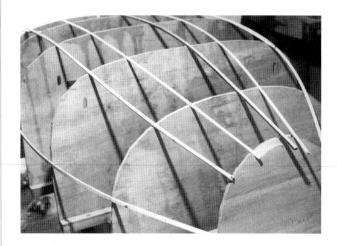

High spots are trimmed a little at a time, until the batten lies fairly on all parts in all directions. The moulds should need little more than shaving off the odd high spot; it is mainly the backbone and sheerline we are concerned about.

4-54

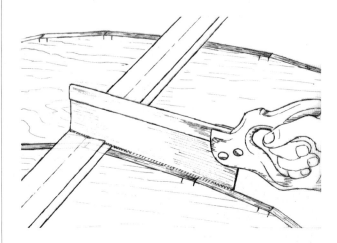

Where more wood is to be removed from the keelson, a saw cut can be made in way of the garboard, i.e. from the CL to the outer edge of the garboard; this establishes the angle to plane down to.

4-55

Likewise the stem: a batten tacked along the plank lands is bent forward past the stem. The saw follows the line, down to the flat forward face of the stem.

4-56

P The flat bottom on the round-bilge prams can curve down at the edges at the bow.

4-57

The batten gives a good indication of how the plywood bottom will lie.

However there are one or two places where the batten may not show exactly how the plywood will fit; mainly the forefoot, where the garboard will twist quite sharply round to the stem, and perhaps the transom if there is a tuck in it. These parts therefore are not fully faired until the actual plank is being tried in place.

4-58

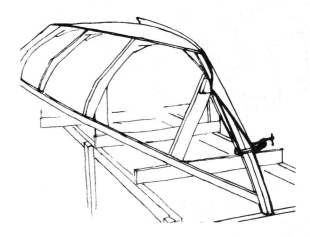

*P*D*DE* With fewer strakes, the batten is laid along each 'chine'. On the wide bottom and/or garboard strake, a scrap of light plywood is good for checking a larger area.

If too much comes off anywhere, decide whether to glue a piece of wood on and fair it back, or fill the gap with thick epoxy. Wonderful stuff. What matters is that the plank will lie fairly, with no air under it.

4-59

The **SHEERLINE** is the most important line in the boat, so needs to be sighted up from every possible angle, close up and from further away if possible. Ideally with battens running the full length of the hull. 1/16" or maybe up to 1/8" - 2-3mm adjustment is acceptable at any mould; much more than that should be checked out from the plans.

Scarph joining the plywood is necessary on boats longer than 8' - 2.5m, although sometimes 10' - 3m sheets can be found.

5-3

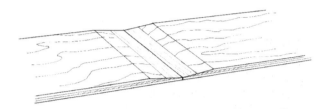

The matching ends of the two sheets are bevelled with a plane, to half the thickness of the plywood. Or a shallow depression is cut with a disc sander. This is filled with fibreglass mat and epoxy, and a piece of 'glass tape laid over it.

5-1

BUTT STRAPS are an easier option, for the simpler dories and prams. They may be thought to look a bit amateurish, but can often be positioned unobtrusively, e.g. under a frame or thwart, or inside a buoyancy compartment. The butt strap allows the builder to use the full length of a sheet of plywood.

The butt strap needs to be 8 times the thickness of the plywood. It is glued and fastened to the first panel, then the next piece is fitted over it as the sheet is marked up for fitting. When gluing the plank, it is screwed with temporary (or permanent) screws, as in Fig 5-40, and the screw holes filled later.

5-4

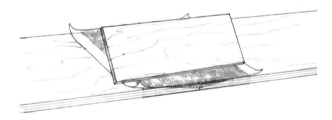

A piece of thin polythene is laid over the top, and squeegeed flat with a wide putty knife or similar flat blade, or piece of plywood. The sheet is then turned over, and a strip of light tape is laid over the joint on the other side.

When working with plywood of 3/8" - 10mm or thicker, the mat-filled hollow can be made on both sides, to about 1/4 or 1/3 of the thickness.

SCARPHING whole sheets of plywood can be done before you start marking out the planks. These can become difficult to manage

5-2

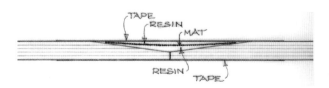

Another option is the **'FIBREGLASS WELD'**, which is good and strong, and is invisible on a painted hull.

in longer boats which require more than two sheets to make up the length, especially if you are working single-handed, and are short of space.

Gluing the scarphed planks on the boat takes a little more time, but you get fairly efficient after a while. I usually do it this way on any boat longer than about 12' - 4m, especially if working single-handed. Refer also to comments on matching sheets, below Fig. 5-34.

5-5

The two adjoining plank ends are planed together after the planks are shaped up. Gluing them up is shown in Fig 5-40.

5-6

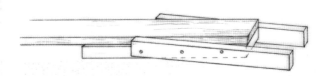

A scarphing jig can be used; this sets the planing angle automatically, and can be used with a plane, planer or router. The width needs to be just sufficient for the widest strake. (This can also be used for scarphing long strips of wood for gunwales etc.)

Two to four whole sheets may be planed up together. They need a flat straight edge under them.

The angle of the scarph is usually 8:1. 6:1 may be adequate, on round-bilge boats with narrower strakes; it will be a little easier to plane. E.g. 1/4" - 6mm ply has a 2" - 50mm scarph (or 1 - 1/2"- 38mm).

5-7

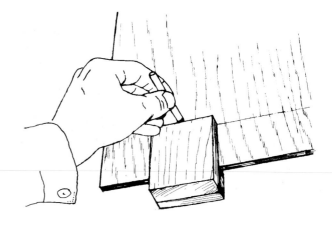

Mark the scarph width with a gauge and pencil.

5-8

Clamp the planks over the end of the bench, with the width marks lined up.

5-9

Plane down to the lines. Keep the plane sharp. The glue lines between the veneers show up any unevenness.

5-10

Ready for gluing.

5-11

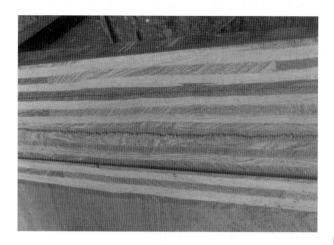

The second plank here had a bit of wild grain on the lower face; it came out slightly ragged. If it will be painted that's OK, but if not, it may be necessary to plane the whole face back a little.

GLUING THE SCARPH on the bench - options:

5-12

Staples can be used with up to 3/16" - 5mm plywood. A strip of ply, of the same thickness or more, and the same width as the joint, is stapled over plastic or tape. A row of staples, along the middle, with plenty of pressure, then one along each edge of the joint. Note the clamps on each sheet, holding them down to the bench to keep them from sliding apart.

Planking

5-13

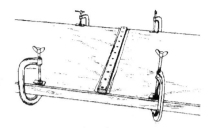

Plywood of about 3/16 to 1/4" - 5-6mm is glued with a batten of about 1" - 25mm, cut to the width of the joint, and screwed down over plastic sheet or tape. The screws are about 3" - 75mm apart. Make a dry run - without glue - to make sure the screw holes are right; if they are too tight it is difficult to get them to pull down evenly. A touch of soft soap on the threads of the screws prevents them becoming permanent. Brush drilling chips away before gluing. Holes will be filled later (- they are not conspicuous if the filler is well matched).

With 3/8" - 8mm or thicker plywood, use two rows of screws, one along each edge.

5-14

Cleaning up excess glue is easier when it is about 90% set, rather than rock-hard. (It may be softened momentarily with a heat gun, but excessive use could weaken the joint). Use a sharp chisel, if necessary. If moving the sheets, or turning them over, take care not to stress the joint.

5-15

Or use a plane, set fine and sharp. (In theory it is best to plane away from the feather edge, but in this case the grain was coming out the wrong way.)

5-16

The spokeshave is easier if the face is not precisely flat.

5-17

But the scraper is the best tool when it will do the job.

5-18

And finish with the sanding block.

A power sander can be useful, but they are inclined to try to remove wood rather than the harder glue.

A slight step between sheets can be planed or scraped flat, but not beyond the face veneer. The cleaning up is less critical if the hull is to be painted.

Gluing the scarphs on the boat is done with clamps or screws; this will be covered when we get to the planking.

FASTENING THE PLANKS - options:

5-19

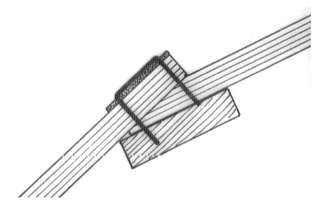

STAPLES in up to 3/16" - 4-5mm plywood. A strip of heavy cardboard protects the surface, and makes it easier to remove the staples. Firm support is needed underneath as the staples are put in; the underneath supporting hand holds backing pads of ply. Sometimes you'll miss and staple yourself to the boat. Ouch!

5-20

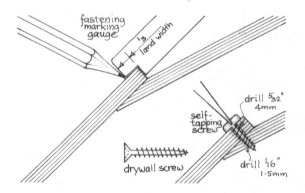

Self-tapping or drywall SCREWS. Self-tappers have a flat head, which does not damage the surface unduly. But need to be counterbored. Drywalls do not, in thin ply; but their countersunk head widens the hole on the surface.

In larger boats, with thicker plywood, and/or where there is much twist in the plank, or using glues other than epoxy, it may be necessary to use longer screws, into backing blocks.

The plank is tacked in place accurately while the holes are drilled. Spacing may be between

2 and 4" - 50-100mm, depending on plank thickness; tending closer with glues other than epoxy.

Experiment with drill sizes on scrap plywood. A variable-speed reversing drill saves a lot of time, especially in a longer round-bilge boat.

Filling all the screw holes later is not very exciting.

5-22

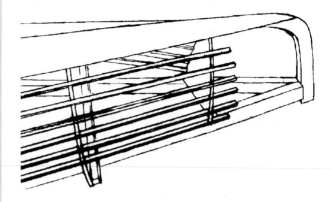

5-21

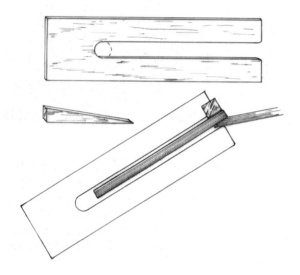

Plywood **CLAMPS AND WEDGES**. Take a bit of time to make up, but are quick and easy to fit and adjust, and leave no holes. Cut from 1/2" -12mm plywood (maybe from mould off-cuts). These clamps can also be useful for other jobs later.

The length of the slots is sufficient for the widest strakes. About two-thirds of them may be about 1" - 25mm less. The width of the slot is twice the planking thickness, or the total of two different thicknesses (i.e. bottom plus sides if different).

Drill a hole about this size and saw down to it. Round off the ends of the slot.

The wedges are easier to use if the faces are planed smooth.

Spacing is around 4 to 5" 100-125 on 3/16 to 1/4" - 5-6mm planks. Up to 7 or 8" - 200 with 5/16-3/8" ply. Closer with 'other' glues. This usually means three or four clamps between each mould.

Tom Hill's **STRINGER** method.

Advantages: planks are clamped to the stringers (except with wide strakes). Bevelling the lands is easier, using a block plane with a piece of wood screwed to its side, flush with the bottom, and resting on the lower stringer. The stringer provides an accurate line for marking out the outboard edge of the strake. They prevent the planks sagging between moulds.

Disadvantages; considerable time is needed to fit the stringers. Dozens of clamps are necessary - unless stapling thin plywood. Cost of the material. Likelihood of unfair lines between the first mould and the stem, in boats wider than canoes (and even possibly canoes - see Fig 5-56).

My opinion: hardly worthwhile for a one-off boat. Very good for production of several hulls. Would recommend extending the stringers through to the stem, joining them with ply gussets, and fairing carefully into the faired stem. Some builders feel it is a safer 'idiot-proof' system. (For an interesting compromise method, see the stringer-fairing system: Fig 5-47/48).

PLANK PATTERNS are needed, at least for round-bilge hulls. Patterns are made for the first three or four strakes, from about 1/8" - 3mm plywood or hardboard. It may be feasible to do without patterns from here on, as the planks have progressively less twist in the ends. Also the plywood sheet is getting smaller, and thus easier to lay over the moulds, and to fit accurately to them. If in doubt, keep going with the patterns, rather than taking the risk of spoiling the planking stock.

In smaller boats, if the planks are to be fitted already scarphed in one piece, the patterns are made long enough by butt joining or scarphing. In some cases the garboard pattern can be used later for the next 2 or 3 narrower strakes, by tacking an extension piece to one end.

The pattern stock is first cut to about 8 or 9" - 200mm wide - the maximum width of the garboard plus an inch or two.

5-23

The pattern is tacked, stapled or clamped to the keelson amidships, just overlapping the centreline, and to two or three moulds, carefully holding it flat at each mould while working aft, then forward.

As you work towards the ends, the sheet is pushed back and forth across the moulds, to find the place where it naturally lies flat on the mould.

If when it is all in place it is not lying flat at any point, the whole end of the pattern outboard must be released and re-fitted. The heavier planking stock will not be forced into place, without creating an unfair line.

5-24

With the fine-bowed Ness Yawl we found that the pattern did not want to sit down on the first mould at its upper edge; the bow had been drawn a little too fine. So it was allowed to follow its own natural line, which was about 1/4" - 6mm off the mould. The same happened with the Acorn Skiff.

5-25

When you have the pattern lying flat on each mould, the transom, and around the stem, it is marked out along its outside edges, and at the plank lands at each mould. The outside marks, don't forget, to allow for the overlap of the next strake. The centreline can be marked with a compass or dividers from the opposite edge of the keelson.

Mark two or three stations so the pattern can be re-fitted accurately.

An accurate fit along the centreline is not important if there is much deadrise, so that the ply will be planed right away at the CL when planing the flat for the outer keel. Refer to the mould patterns or lofting.

The position of the centreboard case can be marked out.

5-26

The pattern is removed, and turned over. The marks are joined up using flexible battens. Follow the marks as closely as possible for a fair line, but if one or two are 1/16" - 2mm out that's OK. As with the rest of the planking it is more important to get good fair lines than to follow the marks exactly.

Try it on the boat, to make sure it fits all round. Also check the fairing of the keelson, transom and stem. It is easier to do this now with the pattern than with the stiffer planking stock. If any more serious fairing is needed, which could slightly affect the shape of the pattern, it can be modified instead of spoiling a plank.

5-27

The stem needs particular attention, as there is usually a strong twist to the garboard here. Now it can be finally faired.

5-28

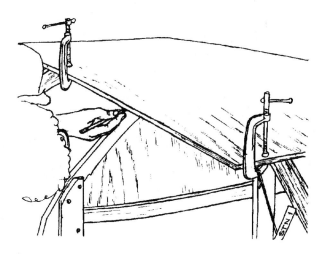

*P*D* You won't need a pattern for the bottom. The bottom plywood is held down flat on each mould, using clamps and/or rope, or shores to the roof, etc. Start at the bow; mark the 'chine' point at each station, underneath. Mark around the stem or bow transom.

5-29

*P*D* The sheet is turned over, and the marks line up with a batten, held to a fair curve with clamps, weights or nails, and the 'chine' line is marked and cut out. (The stick shown is to prevent the batten straightening out towards the end; ideally the batten should extend beyond the end of the curve).

If there will will a second sheet of plywood aft to make up the length, it is marked up in the same way, adding the width of the scarph joint.

5-30

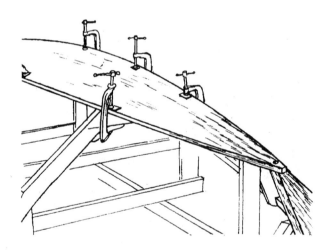

*P*D* The edges are cleaned up as necessary with the plane, and the bottom plank is checked again on the boat.

Glue is spread on all mating surfaces. Including limber holes in frames - this is easier than trying to paint them later. The bottom is clamped to each frame at the chines, and may be temporarily screwed to stem and transom, or held down with weights etc.

If the hull has chine stringers, the bottom can be clamped to them. Without enough clamps, it can be nailed or screwed. Fastenings must be set well inboard to allow for fairing the edges for the garboards.

5-31

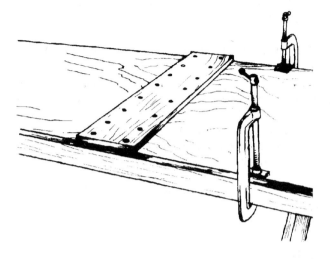

*P*D* The dories' aft panel is scarphed using plywood pads top and bottom - the upper pad screwed to the bottom one. Refer also to Figs 5-39 and 40.

5-32

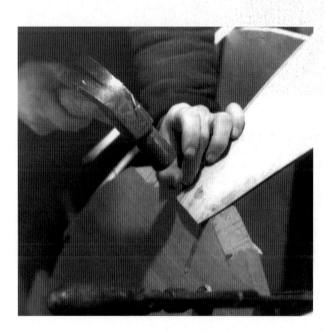

P The pram's bottom is nailed to the transoms fore and aft.

5-33

P As are the subsequent planks.

5-34

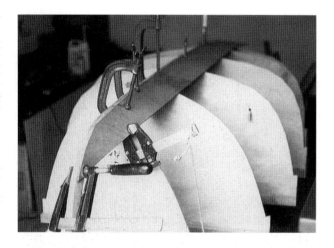

THE GARBOARDS. Before cutting into any planking stock, have a look over the plywood sheets to decide which faces of each sheet will go outside; if the boat is to be bright finished, how scarphed planks will match up. The colour can vary quite a lot even in one sheet. Keep the best looking face veneers for the sheerstrake and topsides.

When planing two sheets to be scarph joined, remember that one of them will be turned over. It is usual, though not structurally necessary, to stagger the joints as far as possible: one towards the bow, the next aft, etc.

A pair of planks is usually cut together. The two sheets are laid together, with the best faces inside, and the pattern is clamped at one edge while the shape is taken off. At least four clamps hold the sheets together; they need to be shifted as the saw approaches, but the sheets must not move. They may be supported on long planks over trestles.

Many builders cut 1/8" - 2-3mm or so outside the line, leaving plenty to spare and having to plane it off later. I am lazy; try to make an accurate pattern and saw carefully, right on the line - erring outside - with a minimum to plane off when cleaning up the edge. It depends a lot on the sawing method: the jigsaw wanders a bit and needs some leeway.

The keel edge can usually be left rough. The upper outboard edge is planed fair.

The first side is laid in place with two or three clamps, lined up with the CL, centre-case, and planks land marks at stem and transom ...

5-35

...then clamped more firmly along the forward part of the keelson, around Station 2. The fwd end is eased firmly down onto mould 1, and around the stem. These two plywood clamps help here; they can be clamped to the moulds.

5-36

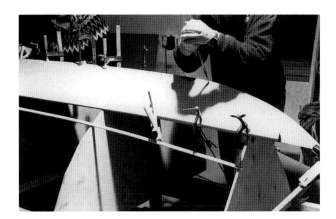

5-37

Over a longer length a batten can be used, with clamps tied down to the building frame. If it is reluctant to come all the way down to the first mould, bring it down as far as it will comfortably come without distortion.

Screws are not essential for strength (the outer keel and stem hold it all together). Ringed nails are usually used at the plank ends up the stem and around the transom.

Some temporary screws may be used where necessary along the keelson, and especially towards and around the forefoot. Best are short fat self-tapping screws, which do not need counterboring; the broad head should not damage the surface. Screws may be spaced about 3 to 6" - 75-150mm. If any permanent screws are used they must not be in the way of the plane when trimming for the outer keel.

Check that the stem is still vertical, and not pushed to one side.

All screw holes are drilled now; nails need to be drilled for also except with light softer plywood. Try a nail in scrap ply. Larger nails in mahogany ply need to be slightly countersunk so the head can be punched just below the surface later without heavy hammering.

Softwood blocks with vee-shaped notches can be used instead of fastenings at the stem, if both sides are glued at the same time.

5-38

Likewise aft, if there is a tuck in the transom (as in the Acorn skiffs).

The plank is marked all round inside for gluing, along stem, keelson, and transom. Several locating marks are made so the plank can be repositioned accurately.

Remove the plank; brush off chips and dust. Tape the moulds etc to keep the glue off.

Glue is spread on all surfaces. Clamps and screws are lightly applied - not tight yet - starting around the 'midships area, working aft, then forward. Nails are hammered in with heads just clear of the surface.

All is now tightened up in the same order. Nails are punched just below the surface. Excess glue is cleaned off, maybe with a putty knife, and washed with a little acetone (with epoxy) or water (with urea or resorcinol).

5-39

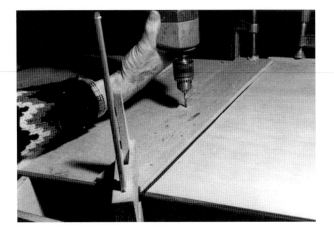

If scarphing a second piece, it is fitted in the same way, adding the width of the joint to its length, and mating the two parts as accurately as possible. They are clamped together with the plywood pads for drilling; the counterbored clearance holes go through the top pad and the planks - i.e. the pads are screwed together; the screw thread does not hold on the planks.

5-40

All screws are driven home but not tight, then all are hardened up.

A plywood hull may be planked up one side at a time, if you are only going to hang one plank in a day. But with enough time and clamps you can do one each side. Either way the planks are cut in pairs.

Patterns can only be done one at a time, working from the previous bevelled plank.

The second garboard strake may need more temporary fastenings, as the first side gets in the way of clamps along the keel. Except in way of the centreboard case, if any.

Glue is cleaned up as far as possible.

Have a look along the outboard edge of the strake; if there are any humps and bumps they can be straightened out with sticks, clamps and ropes, etc.

SECOND STRAKE

5-41

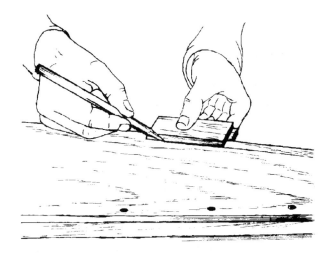

The width of the plank landing is marked along the edge of the garboard with a marking gauge.

Before bevelling the land, the **GAIN** (or chase or rebate) is cut at the bow (*DE*C* and stern) so the the new plank will be flush with the previous one at the stem. The length of the gain may vary from about 8 to 15" - 200-380mm depending on the thickness of the plywood and the length of the boat.

5-42

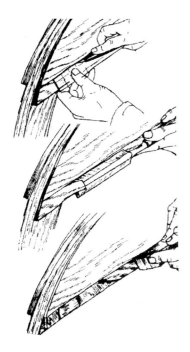

A sharp knife cuts a clean edge, as deep as it can go, forward. The steel rule can be clamped. A tenon saw is used on heavier plywood.

The gain is roughed out with a chisel, finished with a small rabbet plane, and checked with a fairing batten or the steel rule. It is taken down to a feather edge at the forward end.

5-43

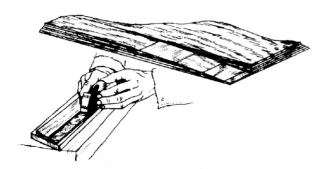

This is done on the boat for the first two or three strakes, because the rebated edge is rather fragile where the end of the plank is twisted. Thereafter however this is not a problem and the gain may be cut on the bench.

Sight up the upper - outboard - edge of the garboard, to see if it is fair. If not, the width of the land may be adjusted, as long as it does not become too narrow.

5-44

BEVELLING - the angle at each mould is set by a saw cut between the inner lap mark on the garboard, and the outer mark on the mould for the next strake.

5-45

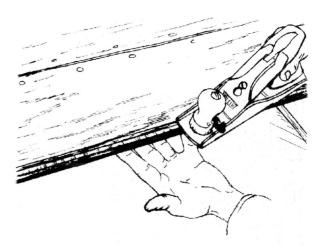

The plywood is planed down to the sawcuts, supporting the ply underneath between moulds.

Planking

5-46

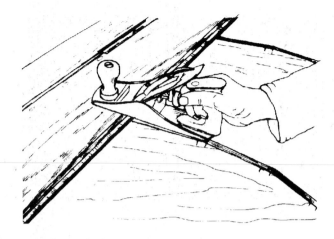

The bevel is checked frequently by laying the edge of the plane on it. The veneer lines help to maintain a smoothly-changing bevel between the moulds.

5-47

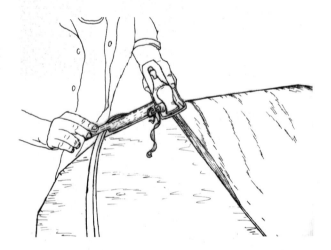

One of the advantages of the aforementioned stringer method is that it gives a dependable way of planing exact bevel angles. This can be done by using a single temporary stringer, tacked to the moulds at the outboard edge of the next strake.

5-48

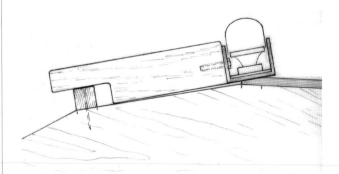

A bar of wood is screwed to the side of a plane as shown, using a short threaded rod with a nut. A step is cut at the outboard end of the bar, the depth of which matches the depth of the stringer.

The stem and transom are finally faired for the next strake. The transom may need to be supported from the floor against hammering.

A pattern is made as before.

5-49

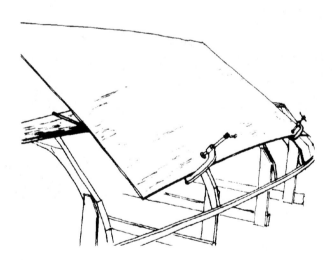

D It may be possible to do without a pattern with wider flatter strakes.

5-50

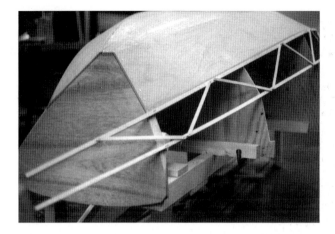

An optional way of making a pattern, using light battens and screws.

5-51

A pair of planks is cut, and the edges cleaned up and checked for fair lines.

Fitted in place; check the fairing along the garboard, stem and transom.

On rowing skiffs with a reverse tuck at the transom one or two strakes will be bevelled at their upper edge, towards the stern, to fit the garboard; refer to the transom pattern.

The scarph is planed if necessary. The operation of the clamps and wedges is tried out.

Nail holes are drilled at stem and transom if necessary.

5-52

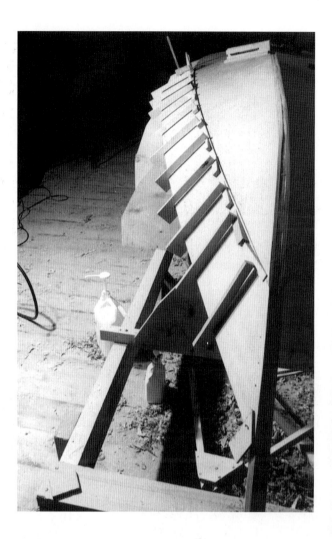

Planks are glued in place. 3 or 4 clamps are loosely positioned; the wedges just tight enough to keep the clamps in place. Check all round to make sure the plank is correctly placed. Then fit all the clamps in the same way, then push all the wedges home. Fit the clamps and wedges just clear of the inner edge, so it will be easier to clean up the glue.

Planking

5-53

When nailing the stem, support the other side firmly. It may be possible to clamp the upper (lower!) corner; if not is is nailed with a ply-wood pad, so the nail can be removed when the gain is cut later.

5-54

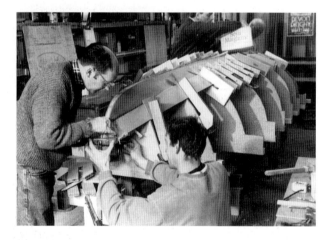

The Acorn Skiff planks are narrower but more sharply twisted.

Look along all edges to see there is a little glue oozing out all the way along. If not, tighten the clamps slightly. Still not? - work some glue in with a putty knife or other thin blade, easing the clamps a little if necessary.

5-55

The screwing method: screws are spaced 2 - 4" - 50-100mm. A thin wipe of soft soap is applied to the threads so they will come out more easily; or, they can be eased out a turn or two, one at a time, then back in, while the glue is still rubbery.

5-56

After gluing a strake, always sight carefully along the edge to make sure it is not sagging between the moulds. If it is it can be supported underneath with sticks etc. Otherwise the hull can finish up looking like this unfortunate canoe. As long as the strake is set fairly the next strake will keep it that way.

5-57

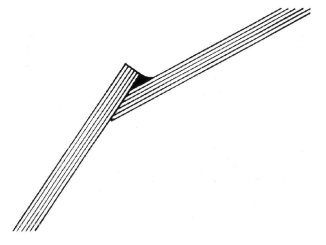

A sharper angle between planks leaves insufficient land width. Plane the bevel down to half to one veneer's thickness, leaving a gap to be filled with epoxy fillet or strips of wood.

5-58

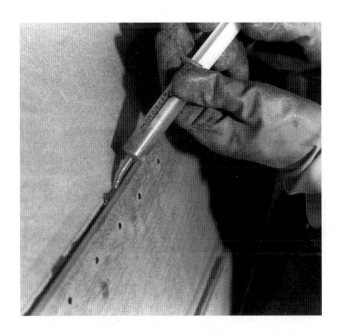

A syringe is useful for filling the gap.

5-59

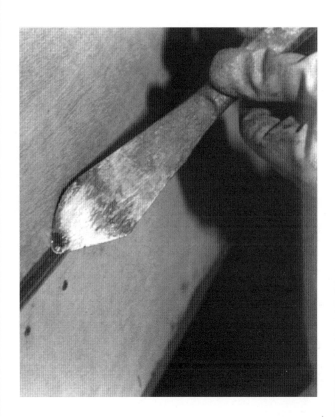

A putty knife with a rounded tip makes a neat fillet.

All surplus glue is cleaned off as far as possible, with chisel and scraper. Some visible glue on the surface is OK, on a painted hull, but all must be scraped away if she is to be bright finished.

5-60

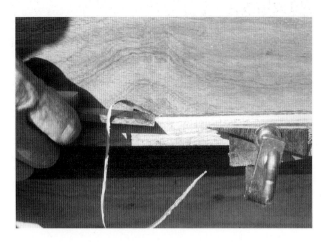

Surplus glue is easiest to remove when it is half-set and rubbery.

Planking

5-61

If it is set hard, a hair drier or heat gun can soften it. Clean off what you can reach inside also. The cleaner you can get the hull as you go along, the less tedious it will be on the big clean-up day, when the hull is planked up.

5-62

The fillet seen in Fig 59 works well, especially in wide-strake hulls. A larger fillet is necessary if it is intended to sheath the hull with Dynel fabric (- see Fig 7-1). Fine-finished narrow-strake skiffs may look better with a clean square corner; this is cleaned up neatly with a chisel. It may depend on whether the hull is to be painted or varnished; if painted, the fillet is perhaps easier to finish. But if finished bright, it may look neater without. Also this eliminates the possibility that the epoxy fillet could be affected by sunlight.

5-63

Finish up with the scraper.

The rest of the planks are fitted in the same way. Patterns may be used for all, or dispensed with when not needed.

Always sight up the plank edges before bevelling a landing or cutting a plank. Follow the marks on the moulds, but don't worry if the fair line means missing one or two marks by 1/8" - 2-3mm.

As you approach the sheer, two or three clamps on the moulds are useful to rest a plank on while fitting it.

5-64

The **SHEERLINE** is the most important line in the boat. It is sighted up from all possible angles, and as far away as you can get, before the gunwale or rubbing strake is fitted. Here it is done before fitting the sheerstrake, with a full-length batten. The lower edge of the sheerstrake will also be highly visible on the finished boat.

If when the gunwale is fitted it will be rebated or have a hardwood strip to cover the upper edge of the plywood, the depth of this strip must be taken off the depth of the sheerstrake.

5-65

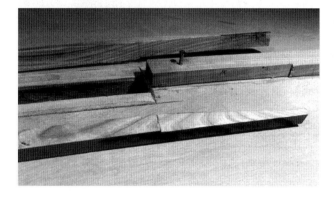

OUTER KEEL components are cut to size, tapered and/or bevelled as necessary, and the inboard ends adjusted to fit the width of the centreboard case.

These parts are held in place while you trace around them; this area of the boat is then planed flat to receive them.

5-66

Forward and aft pieces are temporarily screwed as necessary. The mid pieces are clamped along the centrecase, and clamped to the keel parts at the ends. Without fastenings, it is necessary to get a good close fit with little pressure - and/or close the gap with epoxy.

5-67

This short dagger board case did not need clamps between the ends, as the pieces were sprung down over the slight curve of the bottom. Note the cross piece clamped across aft, holding down both sides. Also the arrangement of clamps forward. (When you can not see in advance exactly how things are going to work, it is necessary to set everything up before applying the glue).

If the centreboard case will later be fitted by the epoxy-fillet method, these side rubbing strips will be fitted later - refer to Fig 6-82.

5-68

The **SKEG** is spiled to fit the keel. It is tapered to its lower edge, usually to about 5/8 to 7/8" - 15-22mm.

5-69

Conventionally the skeg is screwed from underneath, but if not it is simply positioned with tape, then sufficient pressure is applied with sticks and wedges. In this example the stock was not wide enough, so it is made in two parts.

5-70

P The keel can be sprung down with Spanish windlasses.

5-71

A thin piece of plywood cut across the grain can be used to check the fairing of the forward face of the stem.

The inside face of the outer stem is trimmed so it fits the boat. If the lower forward plank edges project out and make the face of the inner stem wider, they may be rounded off to make the width even all the way round.

5-72

The **OUTER STEM** - if made up from sawn pieces, two parts may be assembled before fitting to the boat. Or it may be easier to fit them separately.

5-73

The aft face of the outer stem is then marked to width all the way round.

A centreline is marked on the forward face. I usually run a marking gauge round from each side, which evens out any slight variarions in the width. If the lines diverge, the actual CL is between them.

5-74

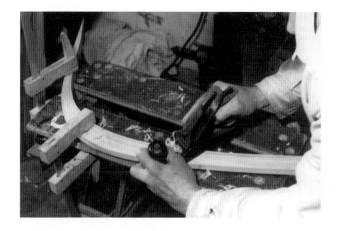

The width of the forward face is then marked and the stem is tapered to this size. The width is taken from the plan, and the corners will be well rounded. Or it is measured to suit a metal rubbing band, plus about 1/16 each side - a little more in larger hulls - 2-3mm.

The top of the outer stem is cut so it will be flush with the sheer - or whatever shape it will be.

5-75

Extra parts around the forefoot are fitted first, then the outer stem is screwed with 10g -5 mm screws, which will be plugged - unless they are temporary.

5-76

This stem fitted so neatly that, using epoxy, no fastenings were needed.

5-77

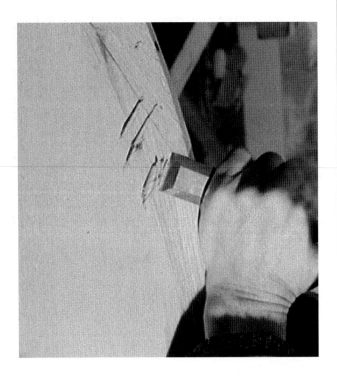

The sides faces are carefully cleaned up with chisel ...

5-78

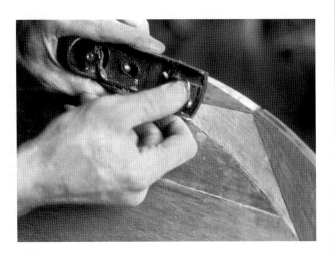

... plane ...

5-79

scraper ... whatever it needs.

GUNWALE RUBBING STRAKES may be fitted before or after turning the hull over. I have always done it before, to stiffen up the sheer, but have seen it successfully done later - on a longer skiff hull where there is less bending stress on it. See Figs 6-6 to 8.

5-80

The pieces are cut to size, and rounded off on what will be the upper outboard edge. The angle at the fwd end is found with a bevel gauge.

DE Likewise the after end. In this case the length will have to be cut exactly. This may be easier to achieve if the rubbing strake is in two parts, scarph joined - which it may need to be to get the length. Each part is glued separately.

5-81

P The fortunate pram builders can simply extend the rail beyond the ends and trim it off later. The ends may extend further and be tied together - see Fig 5-87. (This applies more to the round-bilge prams, which are beamy at the sheer forward, with smaller bow transoms).

5-82

If there is to be a strip added to cover the upper plywood edge of the sheerstrake, the gunwale rubber is set above the sheerstrake. A row of panel pins is set 1/4"- 6mm in from the upper edge; these will be pulled up against the sheerstrake when gluing, to establish the overlap.

5-83

The rubbing strakes are installed in a dry run, to check the fit forward (and aft); to see how many clamps are needed; to mark the sheerstrake for gluing, and to have a final look at the sheerline. In the example here the planking clamps fitted nicely. Start at the bow and work aft.

If the clamps are set just below the edge, it will be easier to clean up the glue in the corner.

5-84

If two parts are scarphed on the boat, a vertical clamp or two can be used to line them up. Check there is no bump in the sheerline where they meet.

Planking

5-85

The ends may be clamped, screwed, nailed as necessary. (See also Fig 6-7).

5-86

A second rubbing strake is fitted in the same way. It is temp. screwed.

5-87

The ends can be tied together.

5-88

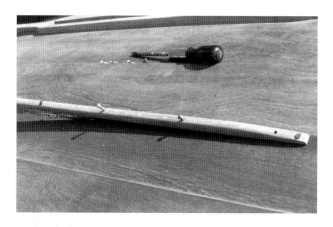

BILGE RUBBING STRIPS are temp. screwed; if there is a strong curve to follow the line of the plank, two screws are put in at one end, and the strip is bent from there.

5-89

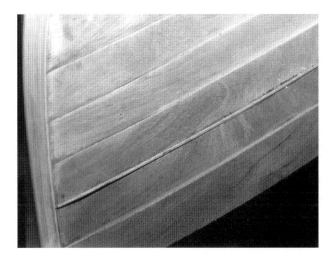

Have a careful look over the whole boat, to see if there are still any bumps or hollows in any of the plank edges. Use a fairing batten if in doubt.

Hollows can be built up with thin strips; (this probably implies a painted hull, unless you use plywood and match it well). The strips are glued with short staples, and trimmed using a fairing batten.

5-90

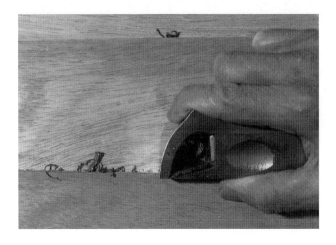

High spots can be trimmed back with a rabbet plane.

5-91

All these screw holes are sealed with thin epoxy, to get into the grain, then thicker epoxy and, if necessary, carved pegs of wood.

Work over the whole boat, rounding edges, scraping clean the last of the excess glue, filling holes, gaps and cracks, and finally sanding thoroughly with progressively finer grades of paper. The hull may be painted, oiled, or varnished now; at least two priming coats will help to protect the surface.

TURNING OVER

The stations are marked in pencil, inside, on the correct side of each mould. Mark them at gunwales and floors, and wherever interior parts will be fitted or measured. If in doubt, mark the stations all the way round.

Some or all of the moulds may be left in, depending on the size of the boat, and the help available for turning her over. They help to keep the hull in shape. Keep at least one amidships and one each end; the more the better. (They will be removed later whenever they get in the way). These moulds are unscrewed from the building frame.

Now she can be freed from the remaining moulds by gently lifting the bow and stern and each side, just an inch, to make sure she is not stuck anywhere.

Now she can be lifted off the remaining moulds and turned over.

Planking

5-92

Usually the hull will be set up again on the building frame. It may be supported in various ways: here sticks are clamped to the frame. Chocks may be fitted underneath.

5-93

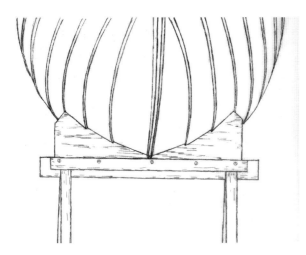

Shaped plywood chocks are more secure; they are made up from the mould patterns. These ones are fastened to trestles.

5-94

This builder disagrees with me about leaving the moulds in. Maybe he's right - they soon get in the way. But they are quickly replaced with these braces, which are notched over the gunwales, and checked once in a while to make sure they stay in the right positions at the station marks, thus maintaining the correct beam dimension at these stations.

5-95

They are useful for keeping the hull aligned; check this whenever installing major parts such as thwarts and knees.

As the turning over marks a significant point in the whole project, the end of the first stage, I always have a small celebration to mark the occasion, and to reward the helpers.

6-1

CLEANING UP the whole interior is more easily done at this stage. This 3-cornered scraper is ground to a different radius on each point. Make sure you do not lose the station marks, at least at keelson and gunwale.

6-2

Inside the stem is difficult to get at; it is cleaned up as far as possible; folded sandpaper

gets into the corners. If it is very uneven a colour-matched fillet up in the corner looks OK, and adds strength. Fairly coarse sand paper folded on edge cleans up the rough bits.

6-3

The sheerstrake edge covering strip - if any - is cut so that it will be just a whisker proud of the sheer and the inner face of the sheerstrake. It can be glued with panel pins, or tape ...

Interior

6-4

or, with the gunwale rubber fitted, the plywood clamps worked in this case.

6-5

Spokeshave and plane are set very fine to trim it flush.

6-6

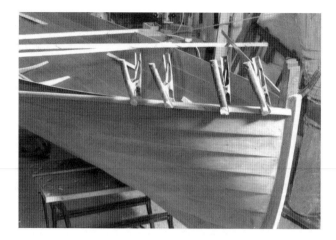

The **GUNWALE RUBBING STRAKE**, if not fitted yet, is lightly clamped in place to check its fit and length.

6-7

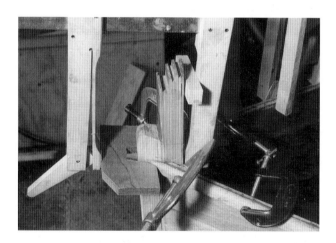

A vee-shaped chock can apply pressure to the ends.

6-8

The faithful plywood clamps may work here also.

6-9

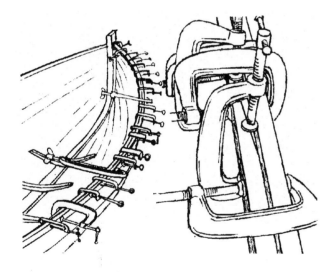

Plain **GUNWALES** (without spacer blocks) are usually fitted before the breasthook and quarter knees, extending to the stem and transom. (See notes re pros and cons of open gunwales - after Fig 6-54).

If a gunwale is scarphed, it may be easier to cut it a little over length, and trim one scarph face until it fits. The forward piece is fitted first, with its scarph face inboard.

If the gunwale is laminated in two layers, they are usually glued in one at a time.

No fastenings are needed, if enough clamps are available.

The temporary gunwale braces will get in the way; they should be replaced where and how possible to prevent the gunwales straightening out. If notched over the sheer, the notches may be widened by the thickness of the gunwale stringers. If clamped, the beam marks will still need to finish up at the inside face of the sheerstrake (representing the beam of the boat, at the relevant station, from the moulds).

Gunwales are bevelled and tapered if/as necessary. The lower inboard corner is rounded off; not the upper corner yet, if knees are to be fitted to the inboard face.

6-10

In designs with a lot of flare, the gunwales are sometimes angled inboard a little, or the upper edge is planed lower inboard, so that it is not sloping sharply outboard. Likewise, if there is tumble home aft, the outer edge of the gunwale may need to be bevelled to bring the upper edge horizontal.

The **BREASTHOOK** in some boats is installed before the gunwales or inwales. If these are plain, without spacer blocks, they extend to the stem and transom, and the breasthook waits until after they are fitted. With open gunwales, the breasthook is fitted now.

Interior

6-11

Start with a cardboard pattern, measured from the construction plan.

Allow some extra width outboard to allow for the flare, especially *DE*D*.

Also allow extra depth equal to the height of the crown, which is usually 3/8 to 3/4" - 10-20mm - greater where there is more flare in the hull sides (esp. *DE*D*). In this case, the inner edges at CL may be bevelled.

6-12

Two halves are cut slightly oversize and offered up. (The forward end may be cut straight across, eliminating the projections alongside the stem and leaving a triangular hole each side.)

6-13

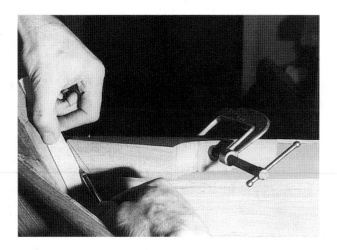

*DE*D* Marking the angle to fit a raked stem.

6-14

A generous sized hole (or two) is bored for the threaded brass rod or dowel, set in epoxy

6-15

The halves are glued together.

6-16

The breasthook is checked for fit, with the top projecting above the sheer by the height of the crown.

6-17

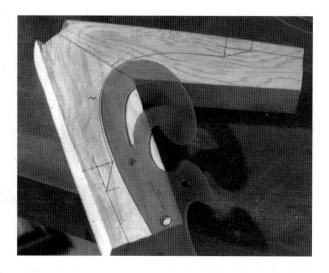

The inside curve is drawn, and the landings for the gunwales measured up. These are cut angled inboard at the same angle as the flare; in line with the sheerstrake.

6-18

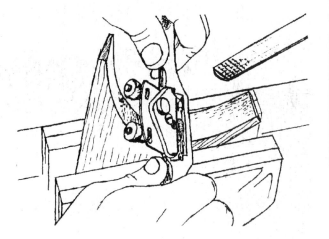

The inside face is smoothed up; it is angled forward so it will be vertical when fitted.

When the crown is shaped, the underside also is shaped so that the after face is a constant depth. Actually it is only the after edge that needs to be cut as it is all that will be visible.

6-19

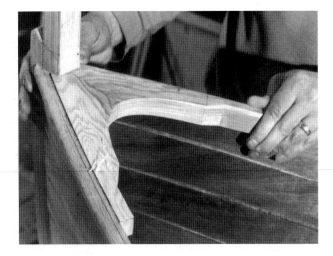

A final fitting ...

6-20

and the breasthook is glued and clamped in place, flush with the gunwale - erring over so it can be planed flush.

6-21

A flush stemhead is planed in line with the breasthook. The block plane is set sharp and fine to deal with the end grain.

6-22

The top of the breasthook is rounded off neatly and is faired into the top of the gunwale.

6-23

The corners of a projecting stem are cleaned up; such corners need particular attention because it is difficult to work and sand along the grain.

6-24

With a rounded stemhead, a few sawcuts make it easier to ...

6-25

... remove most of the wood ...

6-26

... which is finally trimmed with the chisel.

6-27

If the stem is wider than the outer stem it is trimmed to match it.

6-28

QUARTER KNEES are bevelled at the gunwale so they will be angled up about 1/4"-5mm inboard. And bevelled aft to fit the transom.

Laminating if necessary is shown in Fig 4-20.

The step for an open gunwale is cut square, with sufficient width for the landing of the gunwale, allowing for the (near) vertical face to finish up in line with the sheerstrake.

6-29

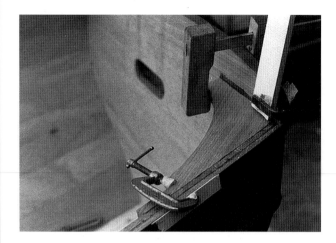

And the quarter knees are glued in place.

With open gunwales and spacer blocks, it is easier to fit them after the knees, which means installing the thwarts now. In some designs the centreboard case is easier fitted before the 'midships thwart; this is covered in Figs 6-84 - on.

6-30

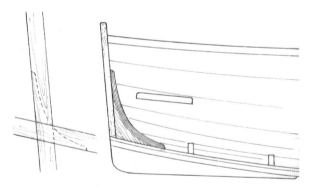

A **TRANSOM KNEE** or sternpost is generally not necessary with plywood construction, but is a good idea if an outboard motor - other than a very light one - is likely to be fitted to the transom. The drawing shows two optional construction methods: a laminated knee, and two pieces halved, as in the stem shown in Fig 4-19.

6-31

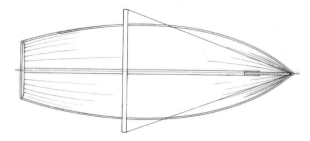

Before installing thwarts, centre-case etc it is necessary to locate the relevant station marks, at least at the gunwales and keelson. If any of them have disappeared along the way, they can be measured from other stations, or from stem and stern, by resting a straight beam across the boat. To make sure the beam is square, a line is stretched from a panel pin forward - and/or aft - at the CL, and the beam is adjusted until the line meets the beam, where it crosses the gunwale, at the same distance from the stem on each side.

6-32

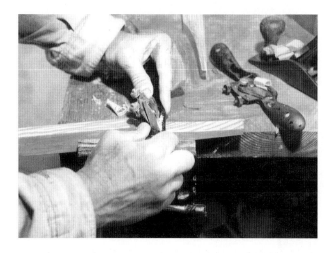

The **'SEATCLEATS'** are tapered to about 3/16" - 5mm at the ends; more in larger boats. They are spiled to fit the hull side.

They are usually fitted perpendicular to the hull side. (Or may be level; this necessitates bevelling the outboard edge to fit the hull).

If they are set low down in a high-deadrise hull (e.g. Acorn Skiff aft) they are bevelled to bring the top back nearer to horizontal. (See Fig. 6-96). (This bevel is the reason for the cut-away ends in the following example; but

square ends look neater, so the ends are left thicker. A twisting bevel can bring the top back to 5mm+. See Fig 6-38).

6-33

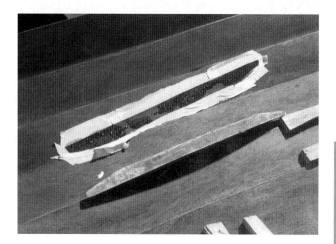

Here the glue is applied to the cleat, which is applied to the boat. The dry spots need a little more. Note the tape.

6-34

Extra big plywood clamps can be made for the seatcleats. Or they may be screwed from outside, with other glue.

6-35

Or clamped sticks may achieve enough pressure, with epoxy. It looks a bit dubious here, as the cleats may move, but it worked.

6-36

With gunwales in place more support is available. Without the gunwales, clamped sticks at the side could do the same job.

6-37

The top surface is cut and planed level to accept the thwarts.

6-38

Check for level top surfaces with a straight edge across the boat.

6-39

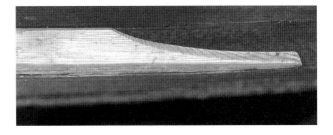

The thwarts usually do not meet the hull side but stop about 3/16"- 5-6mm short of it.

6-40

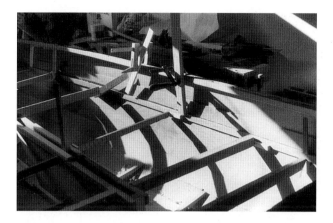

Some boats have a long riser, if they will have decking and side benches etc at or about the lower edge of the sheerstrake. Plywood clamps as in Fig 6-34 are useful.

6-41

It may be doubled in way of thwarts.

6-42

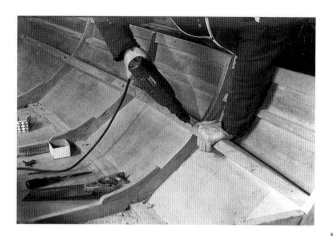

D Dories with frames have a conventional riser screwed to the frames. With built-in buoyancy, the risers only extend to the bulkheads; they may be tapered a little at the ends and be glued to the planking.

6-43

THWARTS are measured with clamped sticks ...

6-44

... and a bevel gauge.

6-45

The ends are spiled for an even gap. (Some boatbuilders prefer to glue the thwart to the hull side. I thought this might be a problem if slight flexing of the side opened a gap by the end grain - but I have not seen this happen yet).

A stanchion may be fitted amidships to support the thwart; this allows a reduction in siding of 1/8" - 3-4mm. It is notched into thwart and keelson. (See Figs 6-95/96/100).

6-46

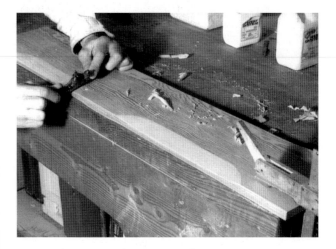

I like to round off the vulnerable upper edges of the thwarts. The underside edges may also be bevelled on light skiffs etc to give a lighter appearance.

6-47

The thwart is clamped to the riser cleats while gluing.

6-48

KNEES are shaped from a cardboard pattern.

6-49

And spiled to fit the thwart and hull side.

6-50

Towards the ends of the hull, the knees will need to be bevelled where they meet the hull; the depth of this angle is added to the width.

6-51

On the inside face this bevel is shaped with chisel and spokeshave.

6-52

The forward knee in beamy dinghies is often set square to the gunwale. This makes it easier to fit the knee to the hull and gunwale.

6-53

The knees are clamped as necessary. Here the thwart and knee are glued at the same time.

6-54

A solution if your clamps are not wide enough.

OPEN GUNWALES take considerable extra time; the spacer blocks must be cleanly cut and smooth-sanded on the end grain; spaced as evenly as possible along the gunwales; glued individually. Painting or varnishing around them is fiddly work.

The advantages are: a sort of traditional appearance, reminiscent of the tops of the ribs in a clinker boat, with the inwale fitted inboard of them. The built-up construction makes the gunwale slightly stronger and/or lighter. A small boat can be tipped on her side to drain the water out, or hose out the interior.
If a design shows spacer blocks but the builder decides to fit plain gunwales, they should be a little thicker - about 1/8" - 2 to 3mm.

6-55

The fancy blocks in some of the following examples have concave ends. These are shaped by setting up a drilling jig.

6-56

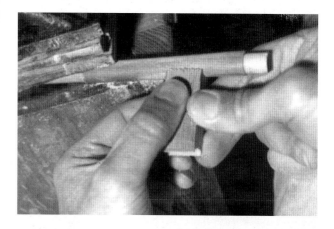

The ends are then sanded with paper wrapped round a length of dowel, and the upper corners rounded off.

6-57

To position the spacer blocks, they are laid on - or taped to - the gunwale and shifted about until the gaps are even, using dividers or a marking stick.

The spacer blocks are spaced out evenly in the areas between breasthook, knees, rowlocks and quarter knees. The gaps between blocks may vary up to about 1/2" - 12mm from one area to the next.

6-58

Oarlock positions complicate the spacing even more; however, in this case, possible variation in the length of the backing block for the side socket gives some extra scope for adjustment.

6-59

The depth of the step in the knee is marked using one of the blocks, along the top and down the sides.

Short blocks may be fitted fore and aft of the knee to make up the length to match the other blocks.

6-60

Or a block may be cut out to fit over the top of the knee ...

6-61

... which is cut off just below the sheer.

6-62

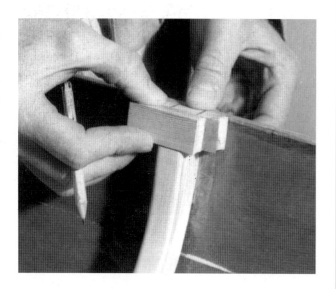

A block is used to represent the gunwale, as the step of the knee is checked; the knee may finish flush with the gunwale inboard, or a little under the edge.

6-63

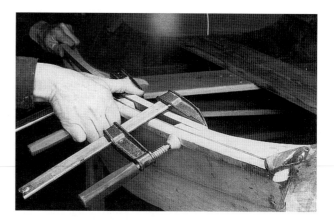

The gunwale stringer is placed hard up into the square step in the quarter knee.

6-64

Work forward, using as many clamps as are needed to ensure the gunwale is in contact with all the blocks.

6-65

The forward end is marked to length ...

6-66

... and cut and trimmed carefully until it fits. Sometimes it needs to be twisted a little forward; this is done using a clamp fitted vertically.

Mark around each block lightly with pencil to show where the glue is to be applied. Glue the gunwales in the boat, starting aft and working forward.

6-67

A scarph join can be done using a scrap block for support. Don't glue it in there permanently.

6-68

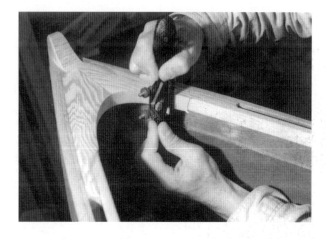

Finally the breasthook and quarter knees are faired into the gunwales.

6-69

FLOORS are spiled to fit the bottom at the appropriate stations, or traced from the patterns. They usually finish neatly at the edge of a plank.

The floors are usually not joggled to fit each plank.

6-70

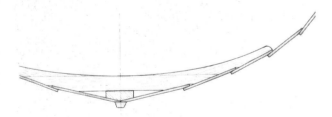

In a flat-floored hull, or area of the hull, the floors are sawn in one piece. In a high-deadrise hull, if the stock is of limited width, extra pieces are glued on to the ends to make up the depth. The grain is angled up a little, which avoids having it cut across the thin ends too sharply. Alternatively, a lamination may be glued to the upper edge.

6-71

The upper edges are shaped with the spoke-shave.

6-72

Floors ready to be glued in. The taping takes a bit of time, but is easier than cleaning up a mass of glue. (These floors are joggled; not doing so is easier and leaves an effective limber hole at each land).

A floor in way of a centreboard case is not glued in until after the case is installed; each half will be notched over the case logs. See Fig 6-92.

6-73

Floors may be screwed to the keelson and plank lands. Or glued with pressure applied with sticks to the ceiling, or to beams clamped across the gunwales - see Fig 6-94. Glue is applied right across the underside of the floor, covering any parts that will be exposed but inaccessible.

6-74

A finished set of floors.

6-75

A **DAGGER BOARD CASE** slot, if not cut already, is marked from the CL, and cut and finished as neatly as possible.

6-76

The parts are all made up.

6-77

The fore and aft spacers are glued to one side, and the inner faces given a thick coat of epoxy. Note the spirit level; the sides are chocked up level so that the epoxy will not flow to one edge.

6-78

Logs are cut to fit; they are glued to the sides of the case. Then they are screwed (if necessary) to the keelson - see Fig 6-90. Otherwise pressure is applied from above - Fig 6-91.

6-79

The forward support piece is fitted to the top rails.

6-80

And glued in place; if more pressure is needed at half-height, a sash cramp is useful; otherwise rope and wedges can do it. The top covering pieces, if any, are added.

6-81

P The wide-bottom prams' case is simpler; stout top rails extend below the thwart.

6-82

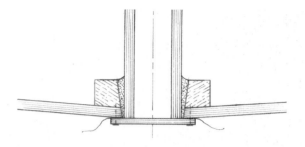

An optional way of fitting the case, in which the slot is easier to cut. With the boat inverted, the slot is cut to the width of the case, erring outside, and the saw is angled a little towards the CL so that the top of the slot is about 1/8: - 3-4mm wider than the bottom.

A strip of thin plywood is tacked to the keel, with plastic tape or sheet over it. With the boat the right way up again, the case is fitted into its place, and lined up vertically, and in line with the CL. Slightly thickened epoxy is worked into the slot, and shaped into a neat fillet. (This is not high-class joinery, but structurally it is perfectly sound).

6-83

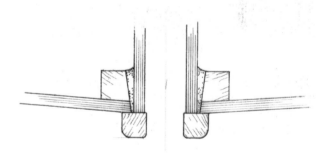

So that the centreboard does not bear on the plywood - there is quite a lot of pressure and friction here - the keel rubbing strip overlaps the edge by 1/16" + - about 2mm.

6-84

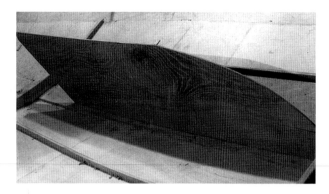

CENTREBOARD CASE procedure is much the same as for the dagger board case. The sides are measured up from the construction plan. The lower edge is cut a little oversize so it can be spiled to fit the keelson. The position of the 'midships thwart is established.

6-85

This set of parts is for the Ness Yawl, in which the after part is curved downwards.

6-86

Keel logs and top rails are glued in place, also spacer blocks on one side only, until the inside faces are smooth-sanded and epoxy coated or painted.

A cardboard pattern of the centreboard - or the board itself - is used to check the fit in the case, using a bolt in the pivot hole. In some boats the bolt goes through the keel logs; in others through short blocks glued on top of the logs. (This case is for the Guillemot design; as it extends partly through the forward thwart, the board will be shaped so it is almost flush at the top when raised - see Fig 6-199).

The sides are then glued together. Clamp lightly at the corners - square up all round - tighten clamps and fit others as needed.

The bolt hole is drilled right through, preferably for a bronze bush. The hole should be well saturated with epoxy.

6-87

Capping and trimming pieces are made and fitted. This case has pieces of ash covering the ply edges at each end. They are tacked in place with panel pins.

6-88

The Ness Yawl's aft covering strips are laminated.

6-89

Positioning blocks are fitted in the slot; they are planed to a neat fit and taped to keep the glue off.

Offer the case to the boat. Get it fitting close; check it will fit in with thwarts etc. Sight up from each end to see it is vertical.

6-90

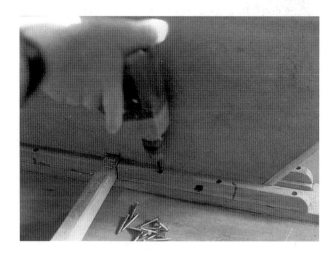

If the case is to be screwed to the keelson, it is positioned with screws at each end, and other screw holes spaced 4 to 8" -100-200mm.

6-91

This case was not screwed; (it fitted fairly well, but needed more thick epoxy than I would like to admit). It was held down by two sticks from above; the beam across the boat holds a vertical piece to line it up.

6-92

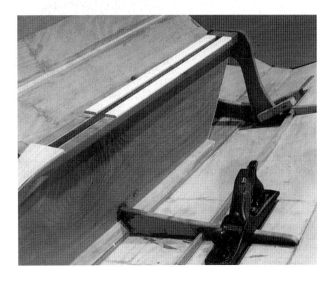

Split floors are fitted. A stick under the top rail can hold the inboard end down. Good fillets here are recommended, as the floor is obviously not as strong as it was in one piece. (However the centrecase makes up for this to a large extent by strengthening the keel over its length).

6-93

DE Some sloop-rigged boats have a mast step fitted to the top of the case.

6-94

DE Stringers may be fitted to the bottom of the Caledonia Yawl, if built with a 3/8" - 9mm bottom instead of 1/2", or to Ness Yawl with 9mm occume instead of mahogany. Limber holes are cut just forward of the floors. They are held down with clamped sticks.

6-95

STERNSHEETS are supported by a beam glued to the transom, and a forward beam epoxy filletted to riser cleats. Note the stanchion notched into the keelson.

6-96

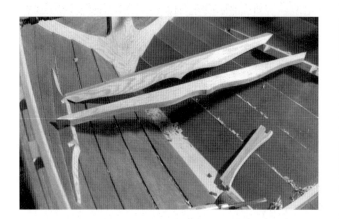

In Acorn Skiffs the sternsheets go further forward. Because of the high deadrise, these cleats are not perpendicular to the hull, but bevelled so they will be nearer to horizontal.

6-97

The ends are cut on an angle, and are notched into the cleats.

6-98

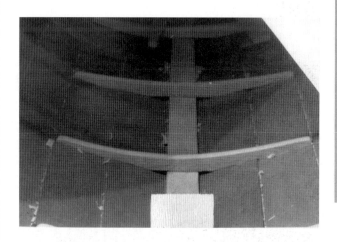

The layout of the boards begins with the central one, lined up on CL.

6-99

When the boards are shaped up from the dimensions on the plan, they are held in place with weights while the screw positions are marked over the centreline of the beams. They are not glued, so they will be removeable.

6-100

Acorns A cardboard pattern is made for the backrest.

6-101

A Small cleats will keep it in place at the bottom.

6-102

A And at the gunwale.

6-103

A This backrest was laminated from two layers of 1/8" - 3mm, with a curve of about 1-1/2" - 40mm.

6-104

SIDE BENCHES extend forward to rest on a cleat which is fixed to the underside of the 'midships thwart.

6-105

Intermediate support, if needed, is provided by a half-beam notched into a stanchion which is notched over the end of a floor, or to a short riser cleat, over a plank land, if possible.

6-106

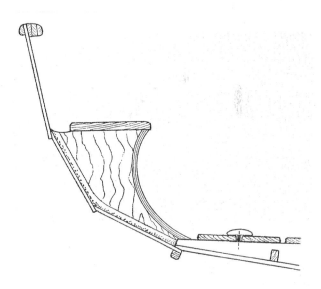

Or by a plywood knee, perhaps edged with a sawn or laminated trim.

6-107

The outer board is spiled from the hull side; about 1-1/2" to 2" - 40-50mm inboard.

6-108

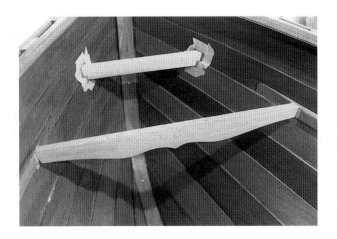

A **BOW SEAT** can be done in a similar way to the sternsheets; the main beam is filletted to short riser cleats; the forward beam to the hull.

(I feel a little uneasy about creating such hard spots against the skin, but the plywood is so tough and flexible it never seems to cause a problem.)

6-109

These boards are sided 1/2" - 12mm; 3/8" - 10mm seems adequate in a light boat.

6-110

P The small Feather Pram's fore-and-aft rowing seat is fixed to the 'mid. thwart, and rests on a block forward, which is fitted to the bottom and the bow transom.

6-111

P The bevel at the forward end is found with a bevel gauge.

6-112

MAST STEPS with an unstayed rig are simply glued (and maybe screwed) to the keelson. An expanding bit is useful to start the hole with a clean edge; but it is unlikely to work its way right through. So unless a hole saw of the right size is at hand the hole is opened out by drilling small holes right around the edge, and cleaning up with a rasp and half-round file. (See Fig. 6-193).

6-113

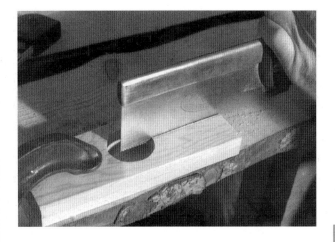

A drain hole is necessary. It is started with a sawcut ...

6-114

... and opened out with saw, chisels, files

6-115

The drain hole is sealed with glue before the step is glued to the keelson.

6-116

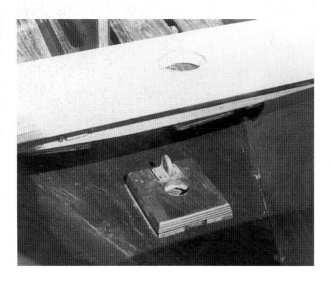

*P*D* On a flat bottom the step is a rectangular piece of ply or wood over a thinner piece each side, leaving a clear space under. The mast rests on the bottom, with glass-epoxy protection.

6-117

With a sloop rig, the standing rigging creates downward compression; in this example the step is extended between the floors.

6-118

When the mast is stepped well forward, or a mizzen well aft, there may be a lot of deadrise in way of the step. And the keelson may be quite narrow, so the step is made wider and faired to fit the garboards. Perhaps notched over the keelson and/or stem.

6-119

The angles are marked fore and aft ...

6-120

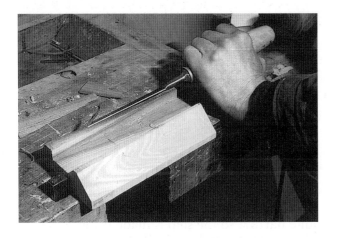

... and cut and trimmed to fit.

6-121

A yawl's mizzen is well raked; drill the corners ...

6-122

... and edges of the hole.

6-123

The sides and corners are rounded and smooth.

6-124

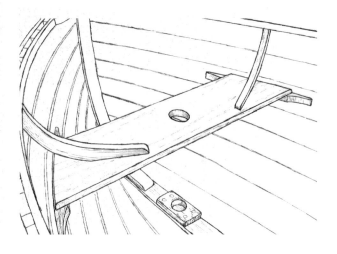

MAST PARTNERS may simply be a hole through the forward thwart.

The hole is made big enough to allow for leather lining to protect the mast; add about 3/32" - 2mm to the radius.

6-125

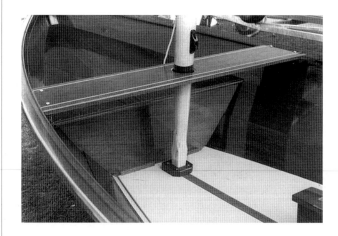

Or a separate partner thwart is fitted at sheer height ...

6-126

... glued or bolted to ...

6-127

cleats under the gunwale.

6-128

The partner may be set up exactly in its place, with the mast - or a shorter 'pretend' mast - in place, vertical when viewed from aft, and at the correct rake.

6-129

The angle is found ...

6-130

... and sawn ...

6-131

... and planed (- this is supposed to be a block plane) ...

6-132

... and trimmed until it fits.

6-133

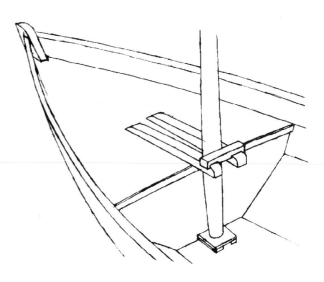

In larger craft, it can be convenient - and safer, in an emergency - if the mast can be stepped and lowered while under way. This can be done with a wedge notched into chocks on a thwart, or deck. The wedge is retained by a light piece of shock cord to the keelson.

6-134

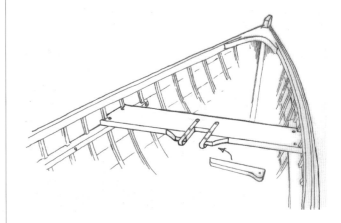

Or the wedge may fit through two U-shaped stainless steel straps. The thwart may be cut out and reinforced with a beam underneath, tapered outboard, or extended aft as shown.

DECKING

6-135

BULKHEADS may be traced from patterns, or lofted on the pattern drawing, or spiled in the hull. Here an undersize scrap of ply is set in place, with stapled pointers indicating the corners. Small scraps of ply are stapled to the bottom and sides on the station.

6-136

DECK CROWN is added if required. If the shape is not given on the plans, the curve can be calculated by dividing the half-breadth into four. 1/4 of the distance from the CL, the height is 94% (or 15/16" to an inch). At halfway it is 75% (3/4"); 3/4 breadth 44% (7/16"). The marks are joined up with a flexible batten. The crown is usually about 1" to 1-1/2" - 25-40mm.

6-137

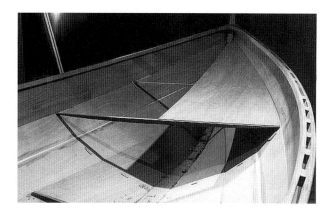

Flat decks work fine and look OK, especially in smaller areas in smaller boats. See also Fig 6-125.

They are certainly easier to make. I'm not sure now if cambered decks are necessary at all (unless they are at sheer height); however they are slightly stronger and also give a little more bury to the mast, if it is stepped through the deck or at the bulkhead.

The bulkhead should be a close fit if the interior is to be bright finished. A substantial fillet - or wood cleats - can support it on the inside. If the hull will be painted, you can have a smaller fillet inside and out, so a less-than-exact fit will not show.

6-138

HATCH openings are more easily prepared before the bulkhead is fitted. An elliptical or oval hatch can be drawn using a pattern shaped for one quarter. (Such a hatch can be stowed inside; a round one can not).

It is possible to use the cut-out piece for the hatch itself, if it is cut neatly. Small holes are drilled with the jigsaw or fretsaw blade.

6-139

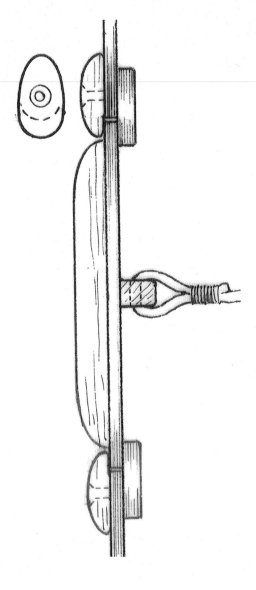

6-140

This is the same size as the opening; it is glued first, and the edges cleaned up, then the wider inner ring is glued.

6-141

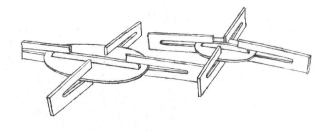

An inner rim is cut, overlapping the edge of the opening by about 3/4" - 20mm. An extra inner rim may be added, to allow for the thickness of the sealing strip.

The hatches are reinforced with a cross-cleat inside, and a vertical one outside - or vice-versa. The inner cleat is drilled to take the retaining shock cord. Turnbuttons may be added for security. Self-adhesive hatch-sealing rubber will be fitted to the rim.

6-142

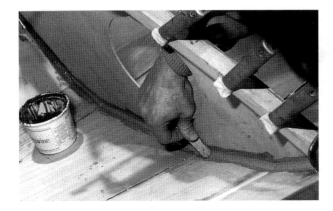

The bulkhead is tacked in place with dabs of thickened epoxy. Some preliminary filletting can be done to use up the excess, but it is easier to do the main filletting when it is firmly in place. Sight up the bulkhead carefully to see it is vertical and not twisted. More stapled pads of ply can straighten it up.

6-143

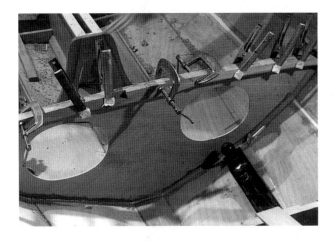

The deckbeam is fitted and glued to the bulkhead, about 1/16" - 2mm proud to allow for fairing. This beam is more substantial than it needs to be for joining the deck and forward bulkhead; it will have cleats screwed to it for halliards etc.

6-144

The **KINGPLANK** is notched into the bulkhead beam, and a step in the stem. It is not glued yet.

In theory you can not get a compound curve into plywood. In practice the kingplank can be curved downwards about 1/2" -12mm. From this you can measure the depth of the other deckbeams, and plot the curves using the same percentages (Fig 6-136).

6-145

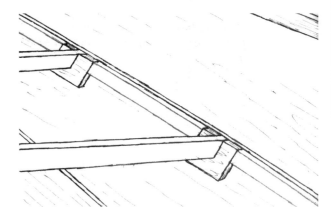

Deckbeams are notched to fit the kingplank, and fitted to the sides of the hull. Stapled pads of plywood set inboard, and underneath if necessary, can hold them in place until the glue sets. Later, substantial fillets are added - or U-shaped pieces of plywood.

6-146

DECKS are usually made in two halves, joined at CL over the kingplank. A cardboard pattern is made, about 1/4" - 5mm oversize. One plywood side is cut and fitted at the outboard edge.

6-147

The edge is trimmed a little at a time; the plane is taking more off the underside to allow for the bevel (due to the flare, if any). When it's getting close, clamp the deck to the kingplank - overlapping the CL - and bend the ply down outboard, adjusting the clamps until it is touching the hull sides at the high points.

6-148

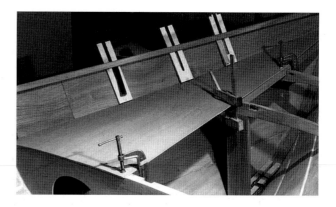

Sticks under the gunwale hold it down. Now the outer edge can be spiled, trimmed and finally fitted.

The ply is bent down to the kingplank, and the CL marked. Trim close to this line; leave 1 mm for final fitting later. Trim to the bulkhead also; leave a whisker over to be finished later.

Use this piece as a pattern for the other side. Leave this a fraction oversize for now.

It is surprisingly easy to get the deck panels a bit too small. A gap of 1/16" - 1mm+ can be quite inconspicuous, if the glue is colour-matched. Otherwise, a contrasting centreline strip looks quite attractive ...

RISERS With 'other glues', risers of about 1/2" to 5/8" - 12-15mm are glued to the hull side at the underside of the deck. They are bevelled to line up with the deckbeams. See Fig 6-40.

6-149

With epoxy, a fillet is made; a strip of 3/16 or 1/8" - 3-5mm ply, 3" - 75 wide, is shaped from the deck edge and stapled to the top of the second strake, and to the deckbeams. The underside and edge are taped.

6-150

The fillet stick is radiused 5/8 or 3/4" - 15-20mm.

6-151

The ply strips are removed; rough edges and spiky bits are rough-sanded. Gaps are filled.

(This system could be more difficult if the deck is not following the upper edge of a strake).

6-152

Try a dry run with the deck panels. Wedge/clamp/staple outboard edges, making sure they are hard down all the way; work down to CL, trimming the inner edge as necessary. These wedging sticks are placed on an angle, and twisted to nearer to vertical to apply pressure. The ends are taped to keep the glue off.

Interior

6-153

6-154

Apply glue, fairly generously, to the first panel. Lay it in place; insert a few wedging sticks lightly under the gunwale. The first side can be lightly clamped to the kingplank; for the second side, clamp a taped flat stick over the CL. Check the position of the plywood. Clamp at bulkhead if possible.

6-155

The decks are all ready to be glued, but any other interior work is done first. Mast steps are fitted. Make sure there are no places where water can rest; it must all be able to run inboard to the bulkhead. Then the whole interior and underside of the deck is epoxy-coated or varnished.

Tape deck edges, sheerstrake and bulkhead.

The decks are normally stapled or nailed; the following method avoids the resulting holes, but is a bit fiddly and may not give sufficient localised pressure for other glues, unless the faying surfaces really fit closely.

Fit more sticks and begin tightening them up, while applying pressure at CL. The bulkhead edge is taped, weighted, or stapled.

Do a dry run with the second side before gluing it, to check the fit at CL.

6-156

Weights can be used, with epoxy. They must be carefully adjusted for even pressure.

6-157

This is a dory deck, stapled with strips of cardboard.

6-158

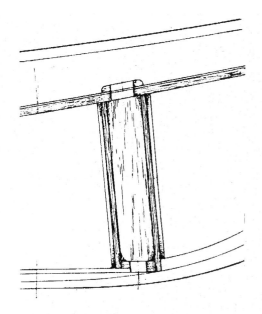

A mast through the deck requires a watertight box, of 1/2" -12mm plywood, or 3/4" - 20mm spacers fore and aft, with plywood sides, all filletted. With a drain tube, maybe of 1/2" - 12mm copper or plastic tube, with the ends well roughed up so the epoxy fillets will stick.

6-159

DE A yawl rigged boat may have a forward mast position, for use without the mizzen. This may be aft of the bulkhead, with wedge and chocks as in Fig 133, or a long box, which makes mast stepping much easier than the hole through the deck.

Mast steps are the same width as the end spacers. Both drain aft.

Interior

6-160

DE Sides are filletted all round. Top rails and half-deckbeams are added.

Note notches in deckbeams for the top rails, which are fitted after the sides. Everything is faired up for the deck.

6-161

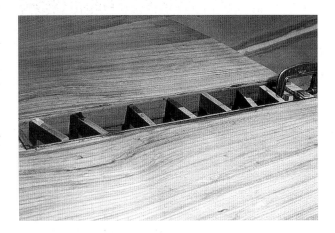

DE When the deck is fitted, bearing strips are added.

6-162

DE And mast chocks.

6-163

BULKHEAD TRIM pieces are fitted to the hull sides. The upper edge is traced from the deck.

6-164

It is glued with clamps where possible, and panel pins. The top edge will be planed flush with the deck. (The sticks seen here are pressing forward from the 'midships thwart.)

6-165

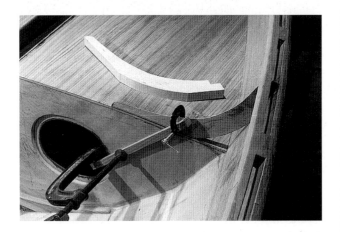

Finally the knees go in. Refer back to Figs 47 etc. Here a thin plywood pattern is made, and the knee is shaped from it - well oversize, allowing for the angle of the gunwale. Having the gunwale in place is making it more complicated.

6-166

Here the relevant angles are marked up, and the forward edge is spiled to fit the deck, while the knee is held vertical - in line with the bulkhead.

6-167

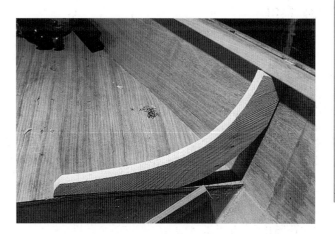

Getting close; the step at the top here must be relieved a tiny bit so the knee can come out and up. The aft face still has to be taken back to fit against the sheerstrake.

6-168

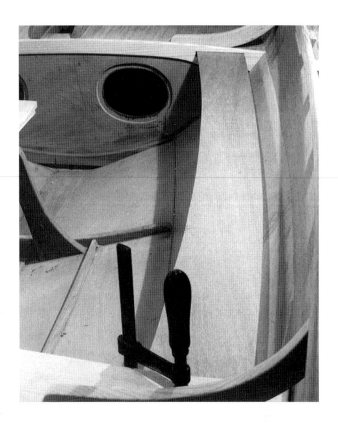

SIDE BENCHES rest on cleats at the bulk-heads, and at the thwart - or may be screwed to the underside of the thwart. See also Figs 6-170 and 6-172.

DECKING OPTIONS

6-169

A half-decked boat (Guillemot 11'-6" - 3.5m). The 3' - 75mm wide side decks are quite comfortable for sitting out, with the low coaming, if/when necessary.

6-170

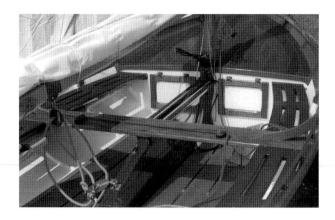

A Gannet dinghy (14'-6" - 4.4m); note rectangular hatches, with brass catches.

6-171

A half-decked double-ender. Note two mast positions, with a sampson post installed in the forward one.

6-172

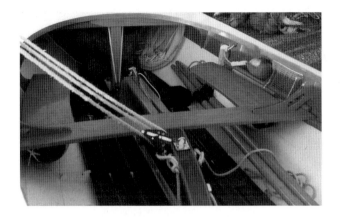

The same boat; she has short side benches fore and aft. Note plywood knees, forward bulkhead, fenders, stowage nets, buoyancy bags.

6-173

An **OUTBOARD WELL** is fitted before the hole in the bottom is cut out.

6-174

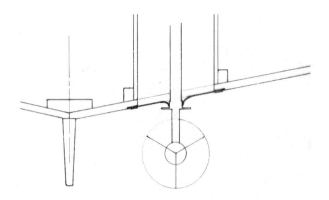

The opening may be closed off with 1/8" - 3mm rubber sheet (From a car accessory store) to reduce turbulence. It is glued with Sikaflex, and slit fore and aft for the shaft. It can be recessed flush with the bottom. A screwed metal strip makes it extra secure, but is not necessary for normal use.

6-175

This plywood plate fits around the shaft. A stick tied to a block jams it in place.

6-176

And/or a box can be made up to fit in the well.

6-177

This is a handy item for light stowage, emergency bailing, peeing in etc.

6-178

A neat stowage compartment for a 3hp Yamaha outboard.

6-179

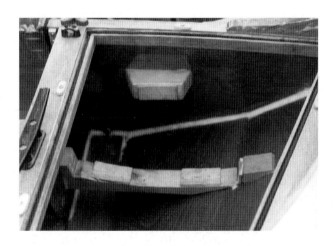

With padded supports for the motor.

6-180

And a well-fastened hatch. Careful fitting, a soft rubber seal, and turnbuttons make it watertight.

6-181

A large deck hatch to fit a light outboard motor

6-182

This one has strong brass hinges and catches.

6-183

A **MAST PARTNER** block is measured from the plans, and drilled.

Interior

6-184

The hole needs to be as round and smooth as it can be.

6-185

It is shaped underneath to fit the deck.

6-186

The deck hole is drilled.

6-187

And the block is glued to the deck.

This mizzen partner has a groove for the lacing of a mast boot. This may avoid the need for a watertight box, but may not be entirely watertight itself.

DE **BUMKIN** fittings are seen above. The block on deck accepts the forward end of the bumkin.

6-188

Inner and outer parts are shaped thus, with a long hole ...

6-189

... which is finally shaped after fitting.

6-190

The two parts protect the plywood edges.

6-191

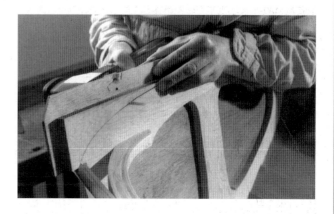

The top of the **TRANSOM** is cut to shape, if it's not done already.

6-192

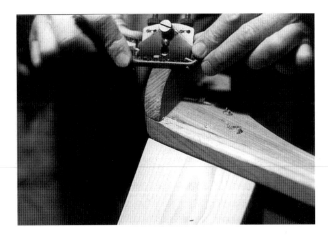

The edge is cleaned up ...

6-193

... and faired neatly in with the gunwale.

FLOORBOARDS or 'bottom boards' will complete the hull. They are usually straight-sided, maybe with the outboard edge curved to follow, more or less, the line of the second or third strake (*P*DE*D* or garboard/bottom).

They may extend full-length, or in longer boats be divided into sections. The layout will depend on centre-case, thwarts etc. The sections may be joined with light battens underneath, maybe laminated with the boards in place.

Plywood bottom boards are an option - see Fig. 6-125.

6-194

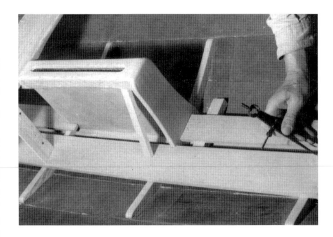

Beginning with the 'midships board, the others are wedged or weighted in place to be marked out. There will be a constant gap between them.

6-195

These boards are quite narrow in a rowing skiff.

6-196

Short centreline pieces sometimes need extra cleats for support. Cleats are fitted to bulkheads also - see Fig. 6-163.

6-197

Turnbuttons are set on blocks on the floors. One usually holds two boards; in this 'midships one a slot is cut for the turnbutton.

The arrangement of the buttons is decided by holding the boards down, to see where they are needed. Two or three turnbuttons in the length of a board should be enough.

In smaller boats it may be acceptable to screw the floorboards to the floors, but at least a short centreline one should be easily removeable for sponging water out. In some boats extra positioning blocks may be needed at the ends.

6-198

ROWING STRETCHERS normally have two or three positions to suit different size rowers. They can be quite plain.

6-199

These simple blocks seem to be adequate in a boat that is not rowed a lot. They are certainly less obtrusive, and are therefore recommended in a boat which will spend much of her time under sail.

Interior

6-200

But a proper pulling boat deserves nicely shaped stretcher blocks; these are often combined with a turned stretcher bar.

(I must say I don't seem to get around to fitting stretchers, and don't miss them. But am inclined to avoid rowing when it is possible to sail).

The final job on the hull is to round off corners and edges; sharp edges are much more vulnerable to surface damage. I like to shape the gunwales, edges of thwarts, top of the transom, etc; all the places the crew are likely to be bumping into. It looks good, is more comfortable, and needs a lot less touching up of the finish.

BIG BOATS

Although getting beyond the scope of this book, the basic construction method for the hull is the same. The difference - apart from the size - is that there is a lot more stuff inside.

6-201

The 19'-9" - 6m canoe-yawl Eun-na-Mara getting her deck and cabin structure.

6-202

A 22'-6" motor-sailer, planking up ...

6-203

... turned over ...

6-204

... and fitting out, with engine installation and cockpit structure.

FITTING OUT

FINISHING

WHAT FINISH will be best for this boat? - and why? - and how is it applied?

A well finished boat will look better, last longer, maintain its value, and be safer. This does not imply expensive imported finishes; simply careful application and maintenance.

If you appear on the beach with a beautifully-painted boat, people will want to know what kind of paint you used. They seem to think that if they buy the same stuff their boat will look as good. In fact she would look just as good if you had used cheap house paint, or anything; they should be congratulating you on doing a good job.

Boatbuilders are inclined to disagree about the best ways of doing things; nowhere more than with finishes. Without going into exhaustive detail, the following are my own ideas on how the various finishes compare, and how they should be applied to the boat.

My criteria for any finish are that it should ...

• Enable the boat to last a lifetime.
• Enhance the appearance of the boat.
• Not require complex preparations or great skill to apply.
• Require a reasonable minimum of time, and energy to maintain.
• Not be very expensive.
• Be pleasant to use.

So the decision as to what kind of finish is best, from the owner's point of view as well as the boat's, is an important one. But even more important is the owner's interest in looking after it. This means an understanding of the material, along with an awareness of its condition and needs. And of what is happening to the wood under it, as the boat endures the very demanding and destructive conditions that constitute her normal working environment.

I find it a source of wonder that such a soft, biodegradeable, natural material can survive so well, compared with modern substitutes. It really does not require a lot of time, just a few minutes' care whenever it is needed.

These are the most popular types of finish:

YACHT VARNISH - beautiful finish - but hard work - thorough rubbing down needed between coats - needs constant attention and maintenance - not durable (but ultra-violet inhibitors now greatly reduce the effects of sunlight).

OIL PAINT (Enamel) - good protection - easy to apply and maintain.

EPOXY - good finish with few coats - tough and impermeable - needs to be overcoated with UV-proof varnish - water can get under a damaged finish - hard to remove.

POLYURETHANE - not suitable for wood boats, except over epoxy primer - too inflexible - poor adhesion.

WATER-BASED 'WOODSEALER' - easy to use - not proven in my experience, but must be worth trying.

EXTERIOR WOODSEAL E.g. Dulux Woodseal, Sadolins - as above; used in construction industry - recommended in magazine articles, which praise its ease of application, but typically say nothing about protection and durability. Which may be doubtful given the small number of recommended coats. Unfortunately contain strong pigments to make sure your wood is wood colour.

OIL FINISH e.g. Deks Olje, Varnol - easy to apply and maintain - excellent penetration and flexibility mean better protection than any of the above (in my opinion) - does not give a high-gloss finish.

These ratings may be taken with at least one grain of salt. Apart from personal

How these finishes meet the above criteria, in my experience:

	durability	appearance	application	maintenance	cost	pleasantness
Varnish	poor	v. good	fussy	poor	mod.	nice
Paint	good	good	OK	OK	mod.	OK
Epoxy	mod.	OK	complex	OK	high	low
PU	v poor	OK	tricky	v. poor	mod.	low
Woodseal	?	OK	easy	?	mod.	OK
Synth Oil	good	good	easy	easy	mod.	OK
Natural Oil	v good	good	easy	v. easy	low	v. nice

preferences, variations could occur in different times scales: for example epoxy could rate high for durability, appearance, and maintenance in the short term - say 3-5 years, but possibly quite low in the long term: 20 years plus. Epoxy and polyurethane look terrible if not skillfully applied. Oil would score high for looks from a distance, but maybe only OK close up, if compared with varnish. Yacht varnish could rate well for durability, as long as it is maintained. (I don't think a thorough comparative durability testing program could be done in less than 20 years!).

PREPARATION

Whichever finish you decide to go for, the most important part of the operation is in preparing the surface. This is much the same whatever finish is used; the only significant difference depends on whether it will be a painted or bright (varnish or oil) finish.

For the painted finish, all you need is a smooth surface. Glue stains, variations in wood colour, minor cross-grain sandpaper scratches, and colour-matched filler do not matter. This saves quite a lot of time in the preparation. But if you intend to varnish or oil the hull, every surface and detail needs extra attention. Scarph-joined plywood sheets should match up as well as possible. It is more important to keep surplus glue off the wood during construction; what is still visible must be scraped clean. Any filler used for nicks and scratches needs to be close to the colour of the wood. Finish scraping and sanding must be with the grain; scratches across the grain which are practically invisible on the bare wood will show up as soon as the varnish goes on. Builders often aim for this standard of finish, and decide later whether to paint or varnish; you still have the choice.

Cleaning up and sanding the main surface areas is easy. What takes time and care are trimming, scraping, sanding all the corners, especially on the interior. All round the riser cleats, knees, gunwale spacers, stem, etc etc. Everything is worked over with progressively finer grades of sandpaper. The grades may vary according to the type of wood; what matters is that you start with something not too coarse, which would leave deep scratches. Probably 100 grade would be as rough as you would need to start with. A usual progression would be through 150 grade to 220 or 240.

I like to work down through about 360 to 600 or 800 grade wet or dry paper. This gives a very fine surface, which when painted or varnished will need a minimum of sanding before subsequent coats. The reason is that, with coarser paper, all the minute hairs and surface roughness left will harden with the finish and will need more sanding before the following coats; obviously much of the priming coats is thus removed. (I think I'm right, but have yet to meet a boatbuilder who does the same). Each grade you use should get rid of visible scratches left by the previous coarser grade.

When sanding along the grain towards an obstruction, a piece of sandpaper may be

Fitting Out

wrapped around a thin flat stick. Otherwise use a flat sanding block on flat surfaces. Power sanders can make it easier; my favourite type is the random-orbital. However it is generally too wide to be very useful on the interior; here a palm sander is handier. I connect these machines to a dust extractor, or at least a collection bag, and use a mask.

Good quality brushes are a good investment, but only if they are looked after. They need thorough cleaning after use, with the appropriate solvent followed by warm water and soap, thoroughly worked in around the inner part of the bristles, then careful drying. Between coats they may be rinsed out with yesterday's solvent, then suspended in new solvent until the next coat. When you find a brush you get on well with, look after it, and will last for years.

I see disposable foam brushes highly recommended, but have not tried them.

The usual brushing technique goes like this: a brushful of paint - or whatever - is laid on, and spread fairly evenly across the boat, over an area of about 2 to 3 square feet - 0.2 - 0.3 sq m - then it is brushed out evenly lengthways. (Brushing only in one direction leaves an uneven coating thickness.) The direction alternates: every other coat is laid on lengthways, then brushed out across the boat. Ideally the last coat will finish up running fore and aft.

However with narrow strakes it may be easier to simply run along two or three strakes at a time, for the length of the hull. Or possibly a combination: coat the edges of the plywood at the lands, spread the paint across 3 strakes for 3 feet or so - 1m - then even it out by brushing fore and aft. The end grain at the laps needs particular attention, but not too much paint, or it will be running along towards the ends and dribbling down the transom. The across-and-lengthways method will be used for wider areas, such as thwarts, transom, decks, centreboard etc.

The area to be done at a time depends on the wet edge. With the lengthways evening-out strokes you will be working away from the wet edge of the previous area. If the paint drags a little here, and leaves brush marks, it is necessary to coat a smaller area each time.

The brush is not dipped into the can; a small amount of the material is poured off into a jar, and the lid replaced on the can, to keep it clean.

Good lighting all round is essential, to show up the evenness - or otherwise - of the finish as it goes on: the brushmarks and runs.

To achieve a good finish requires a dust-free environment. Not easy to do, but the nearer you can get to it the better it will be. After all the construction work it's time for a good cleanup; then the boat is thoroughly cleaned with a vacuum cleaner, then the whole workshop, then the boat. Again. Inside and out.

A light rub down with fine paper can be done when needed between coats, to cut the dust and smooth up the worst of the brush marks and minor bumps. This will always make a difference in the next coat. The surface is always carefully wiped down with a damp cloth or tack rag. I have the habit of wiping each area with my left hand before laying on a brushful; it is surprising how much fine dust is still there. Of course it's always floating about in the air, and coming off your clothes, hair etc as you move around. Vacuum clean yourself, too, in a different room.

With the racing boats we used to prepare for the final coat by sweeping, dusting, vacuuming, late in the evening, then would come down early in the morning, before the wind got up, strangely dressed - maybe in a plastic raincoat and shower cap, or just shorts in hot weather. The floor would be lightly sprinkled with water, and moving around would be done gently. Visitors would not be welcome. It makes a difference, but may be a bit over the top for normal boats.

A good protective finish does not just sit on the surface, but is based on thin priming coats which saturate the wood. Which on plywood probably means most of the thickness of the face veneers, and a long way into the end grain. This largely prevents water penetration when minor dings and scrapes occur. It also greatly reduces the chance of surface checking and general movement of the wood grain. Thus it prolongs by years the time before stripping and re-coating is needed, or possibly postpones this need indefinitely.

VARNISH

Four coats of varnish is about an absolute minimum to launch a boat with. This may be acceptable if there is a positive intention to give her another coat or two before she gets much use. A fairly good glossy finish will need at least 6 coats, and a perfect surface 10 or 12. I start with about 5, and reckon on an end-of-season new coat or 2 to begin really filling the grain. I would like to have it approximately perfect sooner, but can not justify the time it takes. I enjoy sailing more than rubbing down varnish, so do about the minimum necessary for proper protection, and touch it up whenever it is damaged or worn.

Some builders like to use a paste filler on grainy wood before varnishing. This gives you a smooth surface sooner, but I feel it can deaden the lustre and richness of the wood, and may inhibit penetration of the first coat.

The first coat is thinned about 25 to 35%, depending on the wood - less on softwood, more on harder or less absorbent wood. Or follow makers' instructions. The second is thinned maybe 15% or more, then the following coats come straight from the can (jar).

The end grain on the plywood edges will take up a lot more varnish; each time I apply a coat, I will go over the edges at least one extra time before, during and after. Keep working it in as it disappears into the end grain.

A light dry rub over with fine paper smooths the surface between these early coats. But varnish will not stick to glossy varnish, so as soon as a bit of a shine begins to appear, a wet rub down with wet-or-dry paper is necessary. The surface is abraded sufficiently when it remains evenly wet, i.e. the water no longer contracts into globules on the surface. If you're going for the super finish, this is still not enough rubbing to even up the surface; I am constantly feeling it with my left hand to see where it needs more; you can not see how it's going under the water. This can only be done however over a good build-up of varnish, when there is no longer a risk of cutting through to bare wood.

Corners and edges need extra care when rubbing down; it is very easy to take all the varnish off these more vulerable areas (- another reason for rounding them off well). This will not show until the surface is rinsed and dried. Any bare spots have to be treated again before the next coat is applied.

The ideal grade of wet-or-dry to use is the coarsest that will not leave visible scratches after the next coat. But this is not essential on the early coats - you may get away with 280 grade or even a worn 220. But before the last coat you will need about 320 grade.

Touching up during or after the season requires thorough rinsing with fresh water, and drying out. Then careful priming with thinned coats on the damaged area.

PAINT

Many boats are painted outside and finished bright on the interior. Some are also painted low down inside, perhaps up to the ends of the floors. An attractive and popular combination is to also have a bright finished sheerstrake. Or it may be painted a darker contrasting colour.

I was thinking to recommend using 'traditional' colours, but am not sure I could say what they might be. Certainly different things in different places. Bright primary colours are generally to be avoided - however they are seen in France and the Mediterranean. Plain white is practical, especially in sunny climates, but I find it very uninteresting. Just a touch of light grey or cream looks much more distinctive. Certainly these light colours accentuate the lines of the strakes in a lapstrake hull; some builders paint for this reason. For the interior, a pale grey is generally best.

The kinds of colours found in colour charts from the National Trust etc for building restoration work are appealing: muted greens, blues, greys, reds. American boatbuilders often have a good sense of colour; they maintained a much stronger continuity in their traditions than we did. Have a look through a few copies of WoodenBoat, and their catalog.

I like to apply at least two coats of primer (International recommend 4, but that is for boats that live on moorings). The first is thinned up to 20%; I may even add a dash of boiled linseed oil, if the wood seems dry.

Filler is applied at any stage during undercoating. One undercoat is sufficient, but 2 or 3 may be needed if you are aiming for a fine finish. Give it a light rub down between coats, then a thorough one before the gloss enamel. One coat of gloss is a minimum; two is better.

The notes on rubbing down varnish generally apply. But with paint you can use paper about one grade coarser .

Varnished (or oiled) parts of the boat must be done first, with at least 3 coats, before painting begins. Varnish which crosses over the line into the future painted area is easily

Fitting Out

covered by the paint; but paint on bare wood is a problem.

EPOXY

I have never coated a boat with epoxy, so you'd better follow the instructions. If I did it, I would be concerned about getting it into the grain, by either using a thin penetrating primer, or making sure the epoxy and the wood were quite warm. Epoxy is a viscous material, and I don't think it saturates very well - certainly not if it is cold. Increasing the temperature thins it considerably, but if it is a little too warm it goes off too fast. Like suddenly!

Otherwise, you can work over the surface after coating with a heat gun or hair drier; this hopefully thins it long enough for it to start finding its way into the wood. Small bubbles may appear on the surface; this is a good sign, as it means that air in the wood cells is being replaced by resin.

Low humidity is also a requirement, not easily met in winter in the average boat shop.

Epoxy does not brush well, so is usually applied by roller. You need a lot of roller covers. As the roller leaves a slightly stippled finish, it may need light brushing also.

Because of its viscosity and good flowing properties, epoxy gives a good surface with only 3 or 4 coats. But then needs UV-proof polyurethane varnish to protect it from the sunlight. Some boatbuilders use oil paint or varnish, as it is easier to apply and to touch up.

POLYURETHANE - Don't do it.

SYNTHETIC OIL

The best known brand is Deks Olje. It comes in two parts; DO 1 is a very thin oil, which penetrates very well. It is applied 'wet on wet', by brushing on up to 6 coats one after the other, with no waiting or rubbing down. This is continued until the wood is saturated and will take no more; surplus is then wiped of and it is left for 2 or 3 days to dry before Part 2 is applied. This is thicker, somewhere between the oil and normal varnish. It gives a fairly glossy finish after 4 to 6 coats, one or possibly two per day. Again no rubbing down is needed. However I like to give it a good fine wet sanding before the last coat, to eliminate the build-up of dust.

The process is a lot quicker and less critical than varnishing. I find the fumes rather strong. Touching up is dead easy.

NATURAL OIL

The one commercially available in Britain and Norway is Varnol. It has a pleasant slightly tarry smell, which is encouraging. It is applied in the same way as Deks Olje, but comes in only one can. The first coats are thinned with varying proportions of turpentine; less on more absorbent wood. As the absorption slows, the amount of turpentine is reduced. You can stop there; give it a wipe down with a turps-soaked cloth, and it comes out a soft matt finish - which I think looks better than any other finish. But surely gives less protection than the final gloss coats.

Varnol can be very slow to dry; it ideally likes a bit of sun, and some movement of the air. Lack of these may slow down the application of the final coats.

These oil finishes certainly enrich the grain and colour of the timber, and the natural wood ingredients that Varnol is made from must be highly compatible. You'll not get a super-shiny gloss out of it, but it can get close, with rubbing down and careful application of the last coat or two. Personally I like this more natural finish better than super-shiny.

HOME MADE OIL?

American workboats and many small craft are traditionally oiled, where they are not painted. They look very fine when new or re-coated, but the wood sometimes turns dark grey and dull if not kept up. UV protection might prevent this. But when rubbed down and refinished they look good again. Normally a coat or two every year freshens up the finish. I saw an old (80+ years) canoe in Maine, that had been saturated with numberless coats of oil and turpentine. The wood looked so rich and fine, and was almost beginning to look translucent. Epoxy will never look like that, I thought.

However these oil mixtures are generally more permeable than a gloss varnish, so how suitable they might be for plywood planked hulls I'm not sure. It would be very interesting to do some tests with various mixtures. Ask me in 20 years time ...

Here is a recipe for a typical oil mixture, of the kind used in Maine:

8 parts turpentine.
8 parts boiled linseed oil.
1 part pine tar.
1 part Japan driers.

7-1 DYNEL SHEATHING

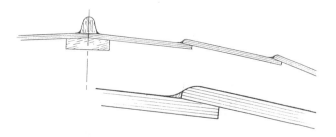

Some builders like to sheathe the bottom of the hull, if it is likely to get roughly treated on pebbly beaches etc, or will be moored. Fibreglass cloth does not work, as it will not lie well over the plank edges; Dynel is softer and more flexible, which means it also resists knocks better. But it can not be clear finished as epoxy/fibreglass can, so will need to be painted.

The edges must be prepared as in Fig 7-1: they are well rounded off and a fillet of microspheres applied in the corner. The left-over mix is used to fill screw holes and any imperfections.

The whole exterior of the hull may be sheathed, or only the area below the waterline. Or, rather than cutting across the edges at the WL, you can sheath the lower three or four strakes. This will also protect the bow for some way up the stem.

Pieces of the cloth are cut roughly to size, then the hull gets a priming coat of epoxy. The cloth is laid on and wet out with a new mix of epoxy, and this is worked in with a brush and/or a rubber squeegee. Make sure the cloth remains in the corners of the laps, and that excess resin is not collecting there.

The cloth leaves a fluffy surface, which needs to be sanded smooth. Or, if you get the epoxy at the right moment, it can be scraped or smoothed up with a fine-set spokeshave. Edges and overlaps can be trimmed at this time.

Two more coats of epoxy are applied.

7-2 THE WATERLINE

A 'dry-sailed' boat does not need a painted waterline, although some owners like to have one anyway. It is necessary if the boat is to be moored for any length of time. In this case the waterline should be about 1" - 25mm above the DWL, to cover the area where surface muck will stick to the hull. Or a boot top of a contrasting colour is added; this is often wider towards the ends of the boat.

The waterline can be marked out with the hull inverted or not, but is easier done when it is still on the moulds. With the height of the WL marked at stem and stern, straight boards are set up horizontally and firmly braced. A taut string between these, moved in and out as necessary, gives the WL at any point. The string may be tensioned using a helper or nails or weights - but it must not sag.

It may be marked with a scriber or compass point about every 2" -50mm. Or further apart, and the marks joined up using a fairing batten. It may be necessary during painting to check occasionally to see the marks are still visible.

7-3

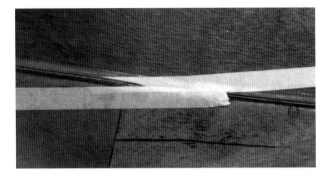

The laps of the planks complicate the procedure a little; the actual level when viewed horizontally runs back under the lap. But usually the painted line runs straight inboard, which is easier.

FITTING OUT

7-4

Half-round brass **KEEL BAND** may be screwed to the keel. A centre punch makes it easier to drill the screw holes.

7-5

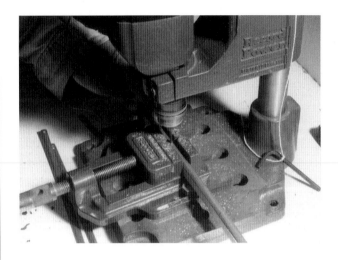

And a jig - which can be made from strips of wood - helps in drilling and countersinking.

7-6

Short pieces are fitted in way of the centreboard case.

7-7

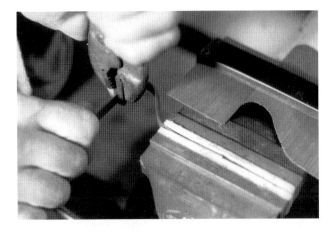

It may follow the shape of a curved stemhead. (The template gauge helps get the shape right - cheap plastic ones are available). Avoid fastenings in bent parts, or drill later.

7-8

Shaping the end finishes it off.

7-9

ROWLOCK SOCKETS - A 'top socket' is laid on the gunwale to establish its position. (This is Daveys' no.1066, seen with a raised pad, as seen in Fig 7-18).

7-10

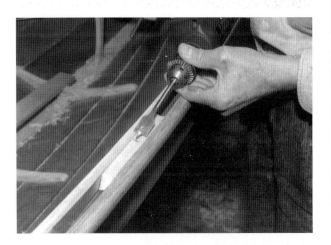

The hole must be placed so that the rowlock will clear the inboard face of the planking.

Fitting Out

7-11

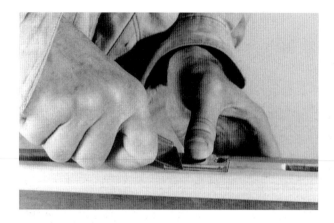

The outline shape is cut with a knife, to give clean edges.

7-12

A router would be useful for cutting the recess; otherwise a drill with a depth marker - I used a piece of masking tape - sets the depth, and the rest is removed with chisels. It should be a close fit, but not tight; it should be possible to remove it later after several coats of varnish.

7-13

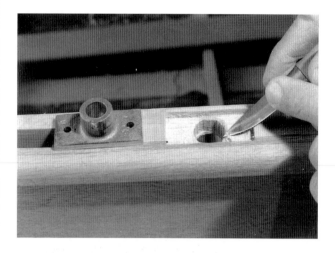

The top edge of the hole must be rounded to fit the shoulder of the socket.

7-14

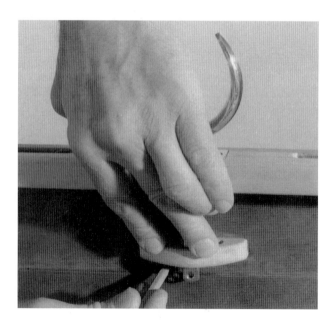

A lower supporting block is advisable, except in small dinghies and prams. Its position is marked out with the rowlock in place.

7-15

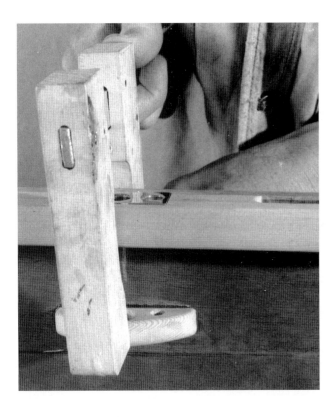

It is glued and clamped; if the clamp is big enough the rowlock can be inserted again to check the alignment.

7-16

The polished bronze rowlocks look fine, although galvanised ones function as well in a workboat. A retaining line is necessary; if spliced neatly around the shoulder - just above the gunwale - it need not be unhitched when removing the rowlock.

7-17

Side sockets are easier to fit. But they reduce the spread of the 'locks. A loop of leather is useful for stowage.

Fitting Out

7-18

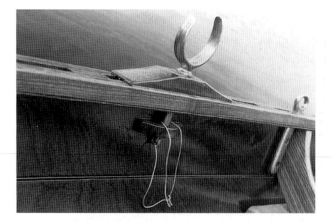

Boats with low freeboard and high thwarts may need pads to raise the rowlocks above the sheer. 6 to 7"- 150-180mm above the thwart is about ideal in most boats.

7-19

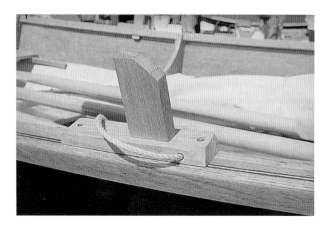

'Kabes' work well in the Shetland style boats. The slot goes right through the gunwale.

7-20

OARS - Flat-bladed oars are the easiest to make; they work well for general use. Proper spoon blades are preferred for serious rowing, but require special planes. The loom may be left square; this helps slightly to balance the oar.

7-21

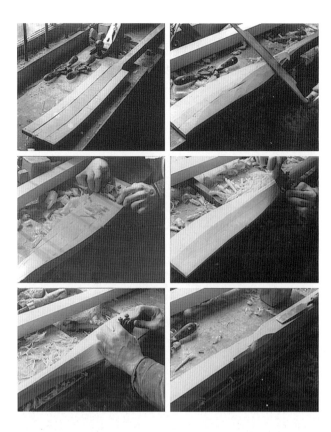

This 'flat-spoon' compromise shape is simpler to build and works very well. The drawknife is not essential; the spokeshave is. The blades are about 28" x 5-1/4" - 700 x 130.

7-22

This builder thought about the grain pattern in the Douglas fir, with no attempt to make it look like one piece. He also fitted neat hardwood tips.

7-23

Leathers may be fastened with copper tacks ...

7-24

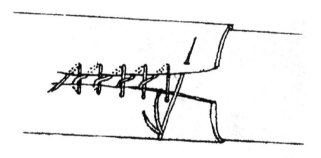

... or stitched.

CENTREBOARDS and **RUDDERS** Two or three edge-glued boards will generally be needed to make up the width. Refer to the comments in Fig 2-3 on alternating grain.

7-25

Layers of plywood are not recommended for a centre- or dagger board, but can work well for a rudder blade, especially if it is a wide one.

7-26

The edges may be bevelled, and the corners rounded off. Side cheeks will be added at the top - either solid or plywood.

A proper **STREAMLINING** job is normally only done with racing boats. But if you are the type who likes to imagine the water streaming past your 'foils' with the minimum resistance, and providing maximum lift when on the wind, here is how it's done.

7-27

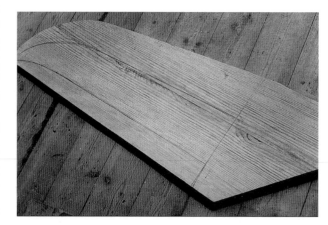

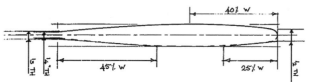

These proportions will give the right shape when the corners are rounded off. The leading edge starts out at half the board thickness; it should not be too sharp or it will stall easily. The after edge finishes about 3/16 to 1/4" - 5-6mm. The area inside the case, when the board is down, remains flat, so it has plenty of bearing surface at the keel.

7-28

Gluing the boards; note three boards underneath to line them up flat. If sash cramps are unavailable, blocks and wedges work fine (see Fig 4-31).

7-29

The marking gauge marks CL round the edges, and the widths of the bevels.

7-30

The bevels fade out at the depth of the keel ...

7-31

... and continue around the lower end.

7-32

Corners are rounded off with plane and spokeshave. You can feel where the bumps are.

7-33

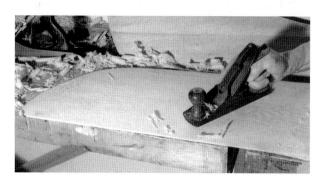

A fine-set plane, working diagonally both ways, does the final shaping.

Fitting Out

7-34

The random-orbital sander makes short work of the finishing; a sanding block, working across the board and then lengthways, does as good a job. (Do not use paper so coarse that it can leave cross-grain scratches.)

7-35

The cleats for the top of a **DAGGER BOARD** are cut away at the sides to make it easier to lift the board.

7-36

The top of the board can be trimmed flush after the cleats are glued.

7-37

I like to round off the corners well, as a dagger board tends to get dumped in the boat and forgotten until someone trips over it.

7-38

A strop of light shock cord holds the board down; it may hook over a small cleat, or a groove across the top of the board.

7-39

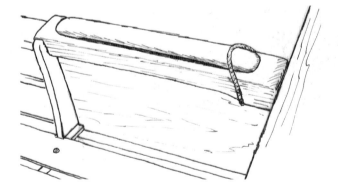

A **PLUG** is generally needed for a dagger-board case, for when the boat is rowed.

LEAD BALLAST is sometimes fitted into a centreboard to 'sink' it, but I find it is never sufficient to reliably overcome the friction, especially when a little sand is present. But it is necessary in **LEEBOARDS** to overcome their buoyancy.

7-40

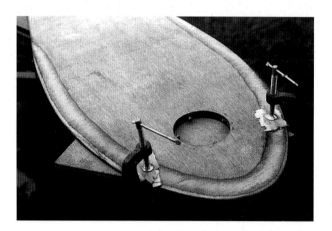

The wood must be dry. The hole is sealed with epoxy. Four screws around the hole will hold the lead in place.

7-41

The board is clamped down on a flat surface, or a piece of plywood is tacked onto the underside. The lead is melted on a gas stove, in a strong old pan, and poured level with the surface, erring over ...

7-42

... and planed flush.

7-43

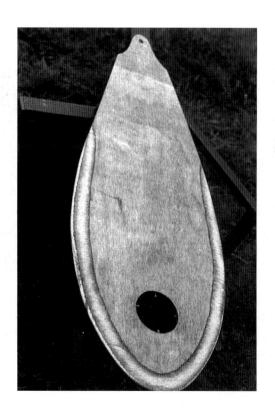

The lead shrinks a little; epoxy is dribbled in around the edge.

A stop is needed to prevent the centreboard disappearing into the case. Wood blocks or a dowel can do it; English dinghies used a pair of rubber door stops, as seen in Fig 6-92.

7-44

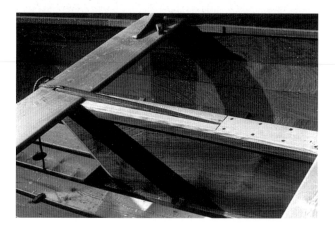

This is not feasible in the Guillemot design, in which the board, being in way of the thwart, is kept unobtrusively low. The lanyard cleats alongside the case, and on the forward edge of the thwart.

7-45

A **STEEL CENTREPLATE** adds some effective ballast; it is usually 1/2 to 5/8" - 12-15mm. Ideally the edges are rounded, and the plate galvanised. Softwood cheeks are epoxy-glued to the sides to make up the thickness of a wood board within the case. The plate is hoisted by a 3 or 4-part tackle from the bulkhead.

7-46

Or led unobtrusively down to the keelson, and aft to a cam cleat - see also Fig 7-113.

7-47

Or a drum winch. The hoisting wire goes round the axle; the line on the drum leads aft to a cleat. This trad. type is made by Daveys'.

7-48

Or it can be made up using plywood cheeks. (This one is made from two porthole rims, with a webbing strap).

7-49

A **LEEBOARD** is retained by a lanyard from a thwart amidships, with a jam cleat for adjustment.

7-50

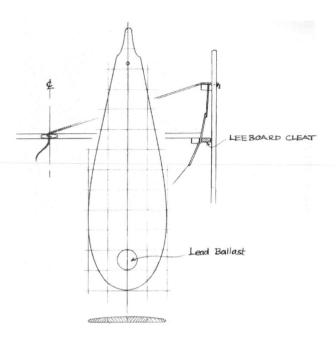

This way only one board is needed. The flat face goes outboard.

7-51

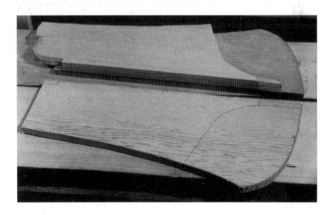

The **RUDDER TRUNK** - or case - sides are usually of plywood; the core is the thickness of the blade, plus about 1/32" - 1mm. The blade is checked for fit and operation; if the lower gudgeon straps are long enough, it may be convenient, and is stronger, if the pivot bolt goes through their after end.

7-52

In larger boats, if the core is thick enough, the tiller may slot through the rudder head. This also may be done with a fixed rudder with cheeks.

7-53

Otherwise, with fixed or lifting rudder, the tiller fits over the head. The notch aft retains the tiller, which is unshipped by lifting the forward end. A wood pin holds it down in use. The height of the tiller can be adjusted by trimming the angle of the top of the cheeks. The tiller should just clear the gunwale when hard over.

7-54

I find it easier to cut the tiller slot cleanly by sawing it out aft, and making a filler block with a rounded end. This block is used to mark the cutout in the rudder head. The block is then clamped in place while the fit on the rudder head is checked, then it is glued in place, as seen in Fig 7-69.

7-55

Rudder straps can be copper rivetted, screwed, or bolted. They may be inset if not wide enough. Seasure black alloy fittings look less traditional, but are neat and more attractive than most stainless steel gear.

7-56

A curved tiller is easily made in two layers; one block under the after end here establishes a suitable curve when the forward end is sprung down.

7-57

Parts of the rudder ready for assembly. Note the hole in the blade with a stopper knot in the end of the downhaul.

7-58

Transom fittings are lined up on CL. One is fastened, then the rudder is hung on it, so the second can be lined up accurately.

7-59

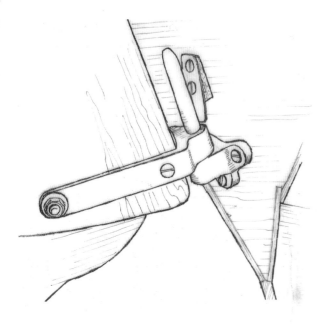

A retaining clip is necessary; the standard stainless ones are fairly tacky-looking. You can make one from a hardwood wedge and a strip of Tufnol, or other hard plastic.

7-60

The whole assembly. Plain well-rounded holes work well with synthetic lines; small sheaves or pieces of metal tube or rod can be fitted to reduce friction. The uphaul goes as high as it can on the after edge of the rudder blade. Lines may lead through the case through the tiller.

7-61

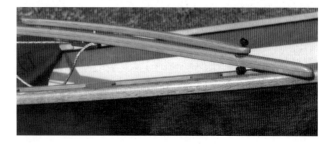

The lines here are actually one, made fast in a jamb cleat. If this is not too tight a fit, it will let go and allow the blade to lift when it hits the bottom. There is a brass washer under the extension.

7-62

The tiller extension with a piece of line avoids another tacky stainless fitting. The stopper knots -seen in Fig. 7-61- get a bit slack quite quickly; the line can be light - about 4mm - and led to a small jamb cleat.

7-63

A fixed rudder is simpler. It gives better control in shallow water, but less in deeper water. After this one hit the sand and hopped off its fittings, the owner rigged a short piece of line with a tube cleat to retain it.

7-64

The handsome cast bronze gear is too heavy for light canoes and prams; these light brass fittings are easily fabricated by anyone with basic metal-working skills.

7-65

A yawl with a centreline mizzen mast needs a laminated tiller. The laminations are bent to their maximum curve ...

Fitting Out

7-66

... and extra clamping blocks are placed as necessary for gluing up.

7-67

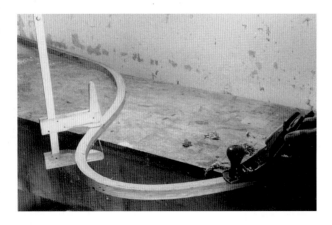

Each half is cleaned up before being glued together ...

7-68

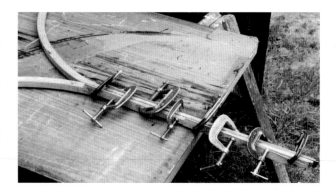

... with the forward end glued straight ...

7-69

... and the aft spacer blocks assembled.

SPARS for these boats are easy to make; finding suitable timber for them may not be. The specified mast diameters assume reasonably clear fir or 'aircraft quality' spruce. If using light pine with some small knots, a slight increase in diameter may be advisable - up to 1/8" - 2-3mm. Not too much - a few mm greater diameter means a significant increase in strength and weight.

Sizes of spars vary with the type of rig. If you do not have a sail plan which gives dimensions of the spars, here is a rough guide.

MAST diameter: about 1:52 of the length above the partners or deck. Down to 1:55 for larger boats; up to 1:50 for small boats. Slightly more for heavier boats. A little less with a stayed rig. (Not much less - although the shrouds support the mast, the compression adds bending stress.)

TAPER:

• masthead is 80% dia. for gaff or sprit rig - 99% at half height.

• masthead is 70% dia. for lug or gunter - 95% at half height.

• masthead is 50% dia. for gaff or bermudan - 90% at half height.

Half height is measured from the partners. The mast is usually tapered below the partners to about 2/3 or 3/4 dia. at the heel or butt.

YARD or GAFF:

Diameter: 1:64 to 1:60 of length.
Taper: heel 82% - peak 62%.

SPRIT can be lighter:

Diameter: 1:80
Taper: heel 75% - peak 60%

BOOM:

Diameter: 1:56
Taper: heel 80-85% - peak 70%

7-70

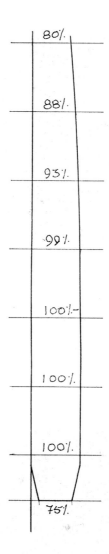

To establish dimensions for the taper, the spar can be drawn shortened to about 18" - 500mm, divided into 4 or 6 equal parts (above the partners), and the intermediate dimensions noted.

7-71

If a piece big enough for the mast is not available, it can be glued up from two pieces. If these come from one board, one part is turned end-for-end, to even up any inconsistencies. They are arranged so that the growth rings are symmetrical. Shorter pieces may be scarph joined, using a ratio of 10:1.

7-72

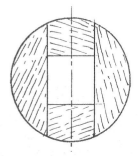

Hollow spars can be made for a larger boat; they save a little weight, and are built up from smaller pieces.

7-73

Spars usually have a straight edge to work from: the after edge of a mast, yard or gaff, and the top of a boom. A centreline is marked on this edge using a string; the diameters at the specified stations are measured from this. (Do not measure from one side, unless the sides are straight). The marks are joined using a stiff batten.

7-74

If gluing two pieces, the taper of the forward edge may be cut first, using a circular saw or bandsaw, and finishing with the plane. Note here how a clear space is left above the clamps, so the glue line/centreline is visible. The spar may be pushed, or even hammered until it is dead straight. (Even bent pieces will stay straight when glued).

The taper of the sides is cut and planed fair, so we have a fully tapered square section spar.

7-75

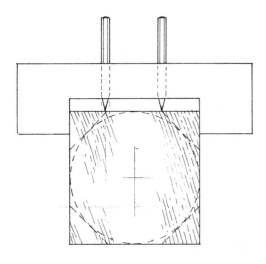

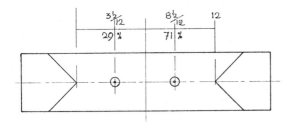

The first step in rounding it off is to remove the corners so it is 8-sided. To mark it up for this we need a sparmaker's gauge. This consists of a piece of wood about twice the diameter of the spar, two nails and two pencils - or biros (which give a clear line and won't need to be sharpened every few feet).

7-76

The nails are held against the tapered side, so the gauge maintains the correct proportions, regardless of the actual width.

7-77

A chock like this, in a vice or nailed to the bench, helps to hold the spar on edge while the corners are planed down. See it in use in Fig 7-83.

7-78

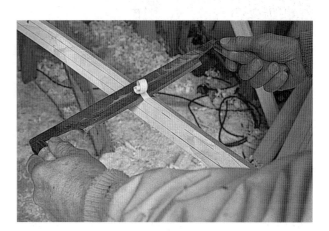

Cutting down to the lines will give us an 8-sided spar. Most of the stock can be removed with a drawknife or electric planer. (But beware - either can very quickly take off too much.)

7-79

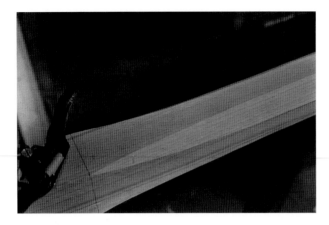

If a mast is square in way of the partners and step, the spokeshave makes the change.

7-80

The corners are again planed off, evenly all round, so it is 16-sided.

7-81

And again. From here on you can work largely by eye, and by working your hand around the spar you will feel the high spots.

7-82

You will by now be coming up against the problem of areas where the grain is running the wrong way, so as you get close to what will be the final surface of the spar, the plane must be turned around in these parts so as not to tear up the grain. The plane is sharp and set very fine at this stage.

7-83

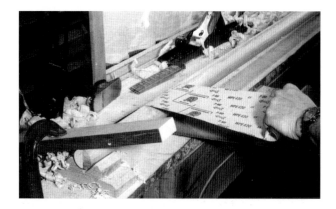

Sanding this way, with part of a belt, fairs off the corners quickly. But it also leaves cross-grain scratches, which will need considerable lengthways sanding to eradicate.

7-84

I prefer to take it as far as possible with the plane, so that only a little sanding is necessary.

I have seen American builders take it about as far as 7-81, and oil the spar without sanding.

7-85

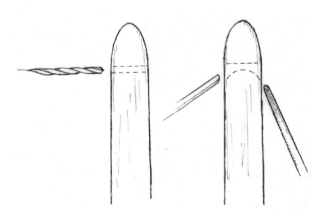

If the ends of the spars are well rounded off, they are less vulnerable to surface damage, and less inclined to knock the boat about when they are unshipped. Holes for halliards and lacings must be generously sized, and well rounded with round files to reduce friction and wear. A dumb sheave for a halliard works well for smaller sails - up to about 65 sq ft - 6 sq m. A slot for a sheave is cut by drilling holes of the same size as the sheave, and cleaning it out with chisels.

7-86

This is a masthead for a gunter sloop rig, with two sheaves for peak and throat halliards, a block on a wire strop for the jib halliard, and leather protection for the mast. The shoulder keeps the shrouds in place, avoiding the need for a metal mastband.

7-87

BOOM JAWS can be simply made from 1/2" - 12mm plywood, set in a slot in the boom.

7-88

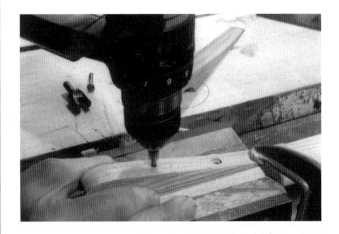

Or built up from a shaped piece of hardwood each side.

Boom ends can be seen in Figs. 7-101 and 7-103.

7-89

They look best if the screws are plugged.

7-90

Gaff jaws are more complex. They are made from layers of hardwood with the grain alternating in different directions.

7-91

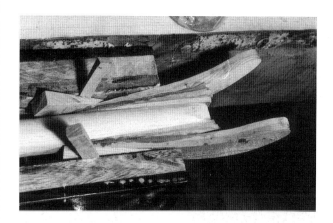

If they are to be screwed, it is easier to get them glued up first.

7-92

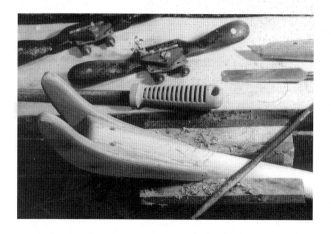

All the corners are well rounded off.

Fitting Out

7-93

Leather lining protects the mast; the two pairs of holes are for the throat halliard and for lacing the sail.

7-94

Parrel beads keep the yard or gaff against the mast.

7-95

The heel of a sprit has a slot for the snotter.

7-96

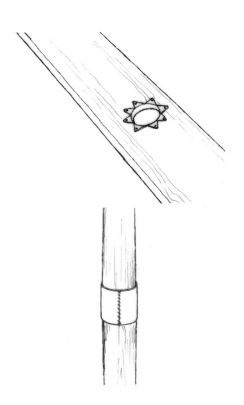

A mast usually has a leather collar at the height of the partners. It may be stitched or tacked. Or the partner hole can be lined with leather.

FITTINGS AND RIGGING

.. vary too much to go into great detail here. There are endless options in the various rigs for different boats, according to the design, the type of rig, particular requirements for individual purposes and local conditions, regional customs, and of course personal preferences.

So the following illustrations show basic standard gear and ways of setting up the most common rigs. They all work, and can be adapted if/as required for particular boats. If you are not sure what you need, look through the magazines at pictures of boats of similar type to your own, find such boats if you can, and talk to their owners. Best of all, if you can make it, is to take a camera and plenty of rolls of colour film to the Wooden Boat Show.

The emphasis is on simplicity; these traditional rigs need very few metal fittings. Wood ones are of course cheaper, often more reliable, and are easily repaired or replaced. Thus avoiding dependence on access to a chandlery, when you're far from home and they're closed anyway.

7-97

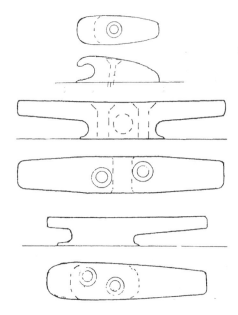

CLEATS etc are usually made of oak. I have also used iroko, ash, and elm successfully. The cleat, jamb cleat and thumb cleat shown are approximately full size for small craft; could be

50-75% bigger for larger boats. Working edges are smooth and rounded.

('Small' refers to boats up to 10 or 12' OA - 3-3.5m. 'Medium-size' about 15' - 4-5m. 'Large' means 17 to 20' - 5-6m.)

7-98

Here is a typical set for a small boat.

7-99

They may be strung up on string or hung on panel pins for varnishing, along with other items.

7-100

Belaying pins look very traditional, and work well for halliards. This boat has a jamb cleat to add versatility.

7-101

Sails are laced to booms, yards and gaffs, with 1/8"+ - 3-4mm line.

7-102

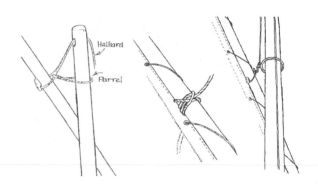

STANDING LUG rig. Small boats have a simple rope parrel to hold the yard to the mast. A medium-sized boat might have parrel beads also. Larger boats use a metal traveller, ideally leathered to protect the mast. The type shown is designed so that with tension on the halliard the ring is about horizontal.

7-103

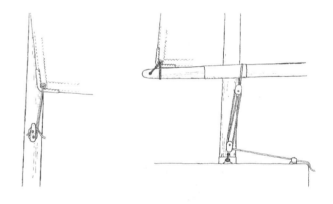

The tack is made fast to a jamb cleat; the tack downhaul runs from a hole through the cleat, to the tack, and back around the cleat.

The balanced lug sail needs plenty of luff tension. This comes from a 2-part tackle in small boats; 3-part in larger ones. A cam cleat offers instant adjustment - particularly useful when sailing single- or short-handed.

7-104

The tackle may be aft of the mast; this downhaul has a snaphook which accommodates different mast positions.

7-105

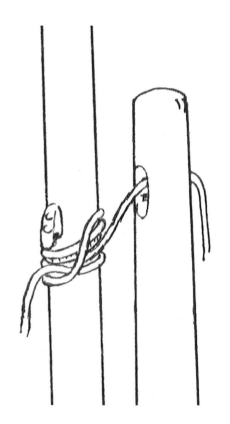

GUNTER and **GAFF** rig. In small gunter-rigged boats the halliard is bent to the yard with a rolling hitch (or topsail halliard bend). This has to be shifted when reefing.

7-106

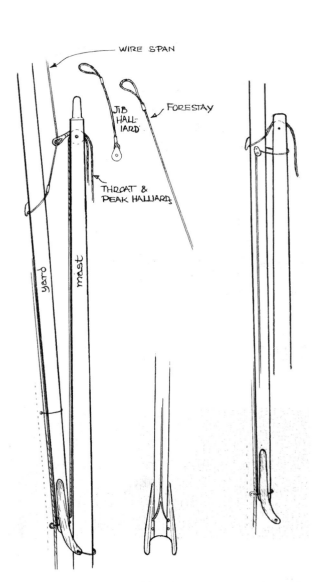

Otherwise, with two halliards, a span is fitted to the yard/gaff. Only the throat halliard then needs to be handled when reefing; though the peak may need adjusting. The same can be achieved with a single halliard and an adjustable parrel; the fall leads to a jamb cleat at the heel of the yard, or possibly to the deck.

Fitting Out

7-107

A bigger-boat gunter rig, with mastband and separate halliard blocks, and a span shackle on a wire span. Smaller craft might use a steel or nylon thimble on a pre-stretched rope span. (Yes that block is capsized.)

7-108

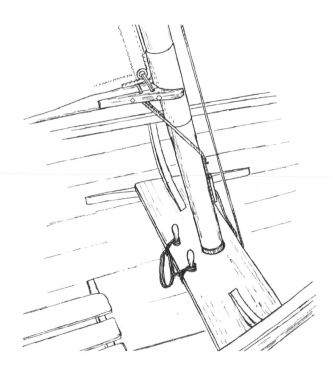

The tack is laced to the boom. This downhaul tensions the luff, and also keeps the boom against the mast. The halliard is belayed on one of the pins, and the coil hung on the other.

7-109

Boom and yard jaws with the sail bent to the spars. The parrel line has a 'slippery overhand' knot (if there is such a thing), so it is easily cast off.

7-110

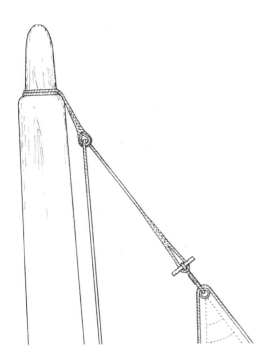

A toggle and a spliced eye can be easier and quicker to use than a shackle.

7-111

A kicking strap is a useful item in a gunter or bermudan rig. It enables the sail to set well before the wind, as well as being much more controllable and safer. Normally it is seriously in the way of the crew, but this type has the upper block on a grommet, which hooks over a thumb cleat on the boom. When it is not needed, i.e. when sailing to windward, and in light

weather, it is simply slipped over the thumb cleat and slides forward out of the way. With boom jaws however it creates friction on the mast; but with well-greased leather this is not a serious problem.

7-112

Jibsheet leads are angled halfway between the directions of the sheet to and from the fair-lead. The hole must be large and well-rounded. In some cases the sheet lead may be a hole in a knee.

Fitting Out

7-113

Mainsheet leads: with mid-boom sheeting, the lower block is on the after end of the centre-board case, or on the keelson aft of it.

A loose-footed standing lug or spritsail is sheeted via a thumb cleat at the gunwale. Or with enclosed fairleads and separate sheets.

7-114

Small craft are not likely to need a metal sheet horse; here is a simple rope one, led through holes in the quarter knees. A figure-8 stopper knot in one end allows adjustment.

7-115

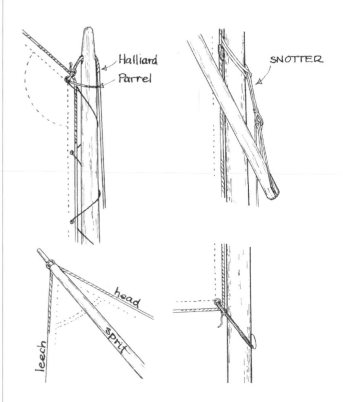

Halliard
Parrel
SNOTTER
head
sprit
leech

SPRIT RIG definitely needs no bought fittings.

REEFING My designs tend to have generous sail plans, for interesting sailing and good light-air performance. I assume sailors have the sense to reef when necessary. Often they don't - or have not bothered to set the gear up. Do it! Experiment with options for your rig. Your boat will be more useful, more fun, more comfortable, and a lot safer. You will not discourage first-time sailors with desperate adventures. Teach the kids. Practice often in light weather, so when that sudden squall appears - as it will - you can keep cool and sail home comfortably, while less seamanlike 'boaters' are floundering helplessly about and hoping a rescue boat will appear. End of rant.

7-116

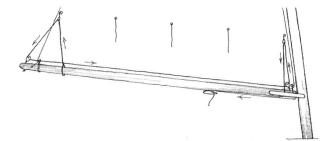

Normal slab-reefing works, but for light open boats a single-line system can be easier and quicker, especially if single-or short-handed. In a larger boat two lines may work better, as the clew and tack downhauls can be controlled independently, and surplus line is more manageable.

Note the hooks, which can be hooked into the tack and clew cringles of whichever reef is required.

With a fixed gooseneck, the line(s) and even halliard(s) can be led aft to cam cleats.

7-117

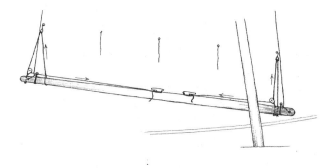

A two-line system on a balanced lugsail.

7-118

The tack of the lugsail. The upper block is not needed in smaller sails (- if at all). With a two-line system, only one block is needed at the boom.

Extra reef pennants are bent to the hooks; they furl the ends of the sail neatly when deep reefed.

7-119

Jamb cleats are neat and quick.

Fitting Out

7-120

Reefing is quick when the gear is set up for it.

7-121

Ness Yawl - comfortably under control in what would be too much wind.

LAUNCHING - after all that work, give her a proper christening/launching party. Decorate her with flags. Tie a bit of tree to the mast, or stemhead. Invite everyone who has had an interest in the boat; let them all have a quick sail, if possible (not all at once). They will all appreciate what a wonderful thing you have created, and it gets the boat off to a good start in life.

BOAT DESIGNS by IAIN OUGHTRED

Designs	Length		Price	
			£UK	$US
Prams				
FEATHER	6'-9"	2,06m	£48	$87
HUMBLE BEE	7'-9"	2.36m	£57	$102
MOUSE	7'-9"	2.36m	£45	$81
GRANNY	9'-4"	2.84m	£51	$90
Canoes				
STICKLEBACK	10'-8"	3.25m	£42	$75
WEE ROB*	12'-0"	3.66m	£54	$75
MACGREGOR*	13-6"	4.11m	£63	$111
Canadian Canoes - strip planked				
BEAVER	16'-0"	4.87m	£45	$78
Traditional Dinghies				
AUK	7'-10"	2.39m	£57	$102
PUFFIN	10'-2"	3.10m	£66	$117
GUILLEMOT	11'-6"	3.50m	£75	$135
TAMMIE NORRIE	13'-6"	4.11m	£81	$144
SKUA	16'-0"	4.88m	£93	$168
Sailing Dinghies / Dayboats				
SHEARWATER	11'-9"	3.58m	£66	$117
GANNET	14'-6"	4.28m	£75	$135
FULMAR	16'-6"	5.08m	£87	$156
Outrigger Skiff - chine/stitch & tape				
SNIPEFISH	15'-0"	4.58m	£51	$93
Rowing Skiffs				
ACORN SKIFF*	11'-9"	3.50m	£75	$135
or	13'-0"	3.96m	£75	$135
ACORN 15	15'-0"	4.58m	£81	$144
MOLE (Thames type)	16'-0"	4.88m	£72	$129
BADGER " "	19'-0"	5.80m	£81	$144
Norwegian Hardanger Faering				
ELF	15'-0"	4.58m	£87	$156
ELFYN	16'-6"	5.03m	£93	$168

Plans

Designs	Length	Price	
Double-ended Dory Skiffs			
SKERRIESKIFF 15	15'-0" 4.58m	£60	$108
SKERRIESKIFF 17	17'-4" 5.28m	£69	$123
Dories			
AMBERJACK	15'-8" 4.77m	£60	$108
JOHN DORY*	18'-3" 5.56m	£78	$141
Double-ended Beachboats			
WHILLY BOAT*	14'-6" 4.52m	£69	$102
WHILLY TERN	15'-2" 4.62m	£84	$150
TIRRIE	16'-10" 5.13m	£99	$177
ARCTIC TURN	18'-2" 5.52m	£111	$198
NESS YAWL	19'-2" 5.84m	£111	$198
CALEDONIA YAWL*	19'-6" 5.95m	£123	$222
Cruising Yachts			
WEE SEAL	18'-0" 5.50m	£225	$411
EUN NA MARA	19'-9" 6.00m	£225	$411
GREY SEAL*	22'-2" 6.76m	£276	$498
HAIKU SHARPIE	30'-0" 9.14m	£330	$594

These are prices for plans ordered directly from the designer in Scotland. Plans are mailed first class or airmail, within a day or two. Prices include inland (UK) postage. Overseas airmail: add £4/$8. Write: Iain Oughtred Boat Designer, Struan Cottage, Bernisdale, Isle of Skye, Scotland IV51 9NS. The complete design catalog costs £10/$20.

US dollars checks are acceptable. Use current price list or current exchange, whichever works to your favor. From other countries, payment can be made by Sterling bank draft, Girocheque, Eurocheque, International Money Order, or by Sterling transfer to Account no. 00123702, Bank of Scotland, Portree, Isle of Skye, Scotland IV51 9EH. Sort code 800947, Acct 00788294. IBAN GB29 BOFS 8009 1700 7882 91. Swift BIC BOSGB21077.

Plans are also available from www.classicmarine.co.uk, and in Australia, www.duckflatwoodenboats.com.

*indicates plans available from WoodenBoat, www.woodenboatstore.com

GLOSSARY

The technical terms associated with boatbuilding vary greatly from one country to another, and even in different areas of one country. However most of these variations apply to traditional construction. I have attempted to offer generally accepted definitions for words that are contained in this book, and my design catalogue, or are otherwise relevant to clinker plywood construction. Noting where necessary differences between British ('GB') and North American ('NA') usage.

(One of my reasons for deciding to do a glossary was my dismay at the degeneration of traditional nautical language that has occurred since I started sailing, and since the advent of fibreglass. Some of what follows therefore is merely pathetic wails of protest, and more or less irrelevant to clinker plywood boatbuilding).

AMIDSHIPS At or towards the centre of the hull.

APRON The inner upper part of the stem, rebated to accept the hood ends of the planking and perhaps gunwales. In glued construction this is usually combined with the lower part of the stem to form the 'inner stem' in one unit.

ATHWARTSHIPS Across the hull - in line with the thwarts.

BACKBONE The fundamental centreline structure of the hull, consisting of keelson/hog and/or keel, stem, and transom, with knees if any, or sternpost in a double-ender.

BEACHBOAT A loose term implying an open boat, without ballast keel, used for sailing inshore or estuary waters, launched from a beach or slipway and hauled out when not in use.

BEAM The maximum overall width of a hull, usually at sheer height, unless there is some tumblehome amidships. For convenience and

consistency I take this measurement to the outside of the planking, but inside any rubbing strakes.

BEAM An athwartships member, usually fitted to support the deck - e.g. deckbeam - or cabin top, cockpit floor etc, or as a spreader between frames.

BEVEL The angle cut along one edge of any part to fit another.

BILGE The curved area of the hull between the bottom and topsides.

BILGE The lowest part of the interior of the hull (where bilge water collects).

BILGE KEEL A short rubbing strake fitted below the turn of the bilge, to protect the planking when the boat is on dry land. (In cruising yachts: a pair of deep bilge keels can replace a normal deep keel or centreboard).

BODY PLAN The transverse vertical sections of the hull, including the transom, as shown on the lines plan. These sections are normally used to provide the shapes of the moulds.

BOTTOM BOARDS or **FLOOR-BOARDS** Removeable boards, usually running fore and aft, fitted into the bottom of the hull above the floors, generally fastened with turnbuttons or screws. (Traditionally 'floor boards' are flat and level; maybe heavier than 'bottom boards').

BREASTHOOK A horizontal knee fitted into the bow at sheer height, tying the gunwales, and port and starboard planks, to each other and to the stem.

BRIGHT FINISH Any clear oil or varnish finish.
BRIGHTWORK Wood so treated.

BUTT Where the end of a member meets

another, or fits into a rebate such as at the stem, or two lengths of planking meet end-to-end.

BUTT STRAP A pad fitted to the inside of two butt-joined planks, made of the same material as the planking, to back up the joint. (Which, even when glued, has very little strength on the end grain). A less professional-looking substitute for scarph joins. (Trad. butt blocks are rivetted, but now are often glued).

BUTTOCKS The shapes of vertical fore-and-aft sections through the hull, used in fairing the lines plan. There are usually two or three in small craft, at equal measurements out from the centreline.

CAMBER *see* **'CROWN'.**

CAPPING A covering piece sometimes fitted to the top of the gunwale and sheerstrake, or centreboard case etc.

CARLIN A fore-and-aft member supporting the inboard edge of a side deck and its beams.

CENTREBOARD A flat board, with rounded or streamlined edges, pivoted so it can be lowered through its case, to prevent leeway and thus enable the boat to sail to windward.

CENTREPLATE A metal centreboard.

CENTREBOARD CASE (GB) or **TRUNK** (NA) A vertical housing for the centreboard, with its top well above the waterline, so as to keep the water out. Usually on the centreline, with a slot through the keel, but occasionally offset to one side.

CHASE (GB) or **GAIN** (NA) The tapered rebate worked into the forward end of a plank so that the next plank up will land on the inner stem, and the outer faces of the planks will be flush at the stem - and the transom in a traditional boat. But not usually in a plywood hull, the planking being thinner.

CHINE The angle between bottom and topsides in a vee-bottom hull. A multi-chine hull may have chine stringers, or be of stitch-and-tape construction.

CLASSIC Traditionally 'Of the first class, of acknowledged excellence ... outstandingly important ...' etc. 20 years ago, when applied to boats, it seemed to mean old - whether any good or not. Now it seems to mean sort of old-fashioned-looking. (Whether made of wood or not).

CLEAT A short piece of wood used for sup-

porting another. Or shaped for making off/making fast/'cleating' a line.

CLENCH To rivet a nail over a rove. Or, without a rove, to turn the inboard end over to prevent it drawing out.

CLINKER (GB) **LAPSTRAKE** (NA) Hull construction in which each strake overlaps the one below it. (Traditionally the planks are rivetted together, or clenched in very small light craft such as canoes). I may appear to be using both English and American terms indiscriminately; have a feeling that 'clinker' seems more appropriate for heavy workboats, and 'lapstrake' for lighter skiffs etc. Which could perhaps make it more appropriate for these relatively lightweight plywood-planked hulls. But I fear this theory has no historic or technical justification.

COAMING Trimming pieces that cover the inboard deck edges, fitted over the carlin, and projecting above the deck to inhibit water from coming inboard.

CROWN The athwartships downward curve of a deck or cabin top from the centreline. May also apply to breasthooks etc.

CURE (NA) In America, glue cures. GB: it sets or hardens. I'll try to get used to this one - along with the computer disk (GB: disc).

DAGGER BOARD A centreboard which is not pivoted, but moves up and down more or less vertically in a short case.

DAYBOAT A beachboat; a large sailing dinghy (NA: sailboat); or an open daysailer, with centreboard or ballast keel, or both.

DEADRISE The angle of the bottom, in section, as it rises from the keel to the turn of the bilge.

DINGHY Generally applied to a small, relatively beamy transom-stern boat with a stem. But may include prams, as well as tenders, etc. GB - also refers to racing centreboard boats. (NA - I have it on dubious authority that it refers to a boat permanently ashore with flowers growing in it).

DISPLACEMENT The weight of water displaced by a boat. Stating the obvious - but confusion is caused these days by many manufacturers referring to the weight of a boat, without crew, gear and stores, as displacement. A practice condoned indiscriminately by most of if not all the magazines.

DORY (NA) A fishing boat with a narrow flat bottom, long ends, a very narrow strongly raked transom, and a strong sheer. Banks dories were carried on the big fishing schooners; they are flat-sided. Swampscott dories were used inshore; they have rounded lapstrake sides with three strakes. Extraordinarily able sea boats. The modern plywood 'light dory' was invented by Phil Bolger with his Gloucester Light Dory - a real classic.

DRY RUN Parts ready to be glued are sometimes assembled first without the glue, to make sure they will go together as intended, and to check that clamping and/or fastening arrangements will work.

EDGE SET When a plank is bent across its width. This can be done in carvel construction, but not in clinker, beyond a very few millimetres, without causing distortion which will prevent the plank resting flat on the mould. (It will want to lift off the mould at the edge away from which it is edge-set).

ENTRY The underwater forebody. A hull is said to have a fine or easy entry if the waterline in plan forms a sharp angle, and/or if the stem meets the waterline in profile at a shallow angle (as opposed to a straight stem). A well-balanced hull, (unlike e.g. a racing dinghy), will be fine-lined aft also, and may be called fine-ended. A full-ended hull has plenty of buoyancy in the entry and in the run. (Not 'exit' please).

FAERING Norwegian four-oared double-ended boat, usually with three or four strakes to a side; lightly framed and flexible. Directly descended from Viking boats, and virtually unchanged in construction. Traditionally built by eye without moulds or plans.

FAIRING Using flexible battens to ensure that all the lines on a lines plan or lofted drawing are fair in themselves and correspond with each other. Trimming the backbone, moulds, frames if any etc in preparation for fitting the planking. Battens of varying thicknesses are used to discover high and low spots.

FAIRING BATTEN A thin flexible batten used in the fairing process to make sure the planks will lie fairly.

FALSE STEM A separate outer stem, fitted after planking. A false keel likewise forms a rubbing strip.

FASTENINGS (GB) or **FASTENERS** (NA) Any devices used to hold pieces of wood together permanently, or to attach fittings: nails, screws, rivets, staples, bolts, and treenails.

FLARE The increase in beam from the turn of the bilge to the sheer.

FAYING SURFACES The surfaces where two parts meet, when they are fitted ready to be glued or fastened together.

FLOORS Transverse members fitted across the keelson to strengthen the bottom area of the hull.

FLOORBOARDS see **BOTTOM BOARDS**. Generally rest on the floors.

FOREFOOT The lower underwater part of the stem as it curves aft into the keel.

FRAMES Transverse timbers supporting the planking, stiffening the hull, or providing support for bulkheads, thwart risers etc. Most lapstrake plywood hulls have little or no framing. (Trad.: also applies to the thin steamed ribs or 'timbers' fitted after planking).

FRONT Ignorant landlubbers' or yuppie boaters' term for the bow of a boat. Likewise 'back'. (Becoming alarmingly common - beware!)

GARBOARD The first strake on the hull; the one fastened to the keel.

GIRTH The distance around the sides and bottom of the hull, amidships, measured from gunwale to gunwale.

GRID The basis of the lines plan, consisting of: in profile, the vertical sections and the waterlines. In the plan view: the centreline, sections, and fore-and-aft buttock lines. For the body plan: the centreline, waterlines, buttocks and diagonals. If the boat has to be lofted full-size, the grid will be drawn on the floor.

GRIPFAST (GB) or **HOLDFAST** (NA) **NAILS** Flat-headed bronze nails with annular rings which greatly increase holding power. Especially in hardwoods, from which they usually can not be removed before the head pulls off or through.

GUDGEON A rudder fitting, fastened to either hull or rudder, with a hole to take a pintle.

GUNWALE The top of the topsides. The whole structure of fore-and-aft members at the sheer. May at a pinch be spelled gun'l, but not gunnel, although that is how it is pronounced.

GUNWALES The main structural members running fore and aft at the sheer, in an open boat. Usually inboard of the sheerstrake. In clinker plywood, they may be separated from the sheerstrake by spacer blocks, giving a sort of traditional appearance reminiscent of the way a trad. boat's gunwales are fitted inboard of the ribs. If the gunwale consists of equal size pieces inboard and outboard of the sheerstrake, the inner one is called an inwale. (But there's no such thing as an outwale). Some light dories, prams etc have a single-part gunwale outboard.

GUNWALE RUBBER/RUBBING STRAKE (GB) or **GUARDRAIL** (NA)   Hardwood strips fitted to the upper edge of the sheerstrake, outboard, for protection.

GUNWHALE There's blue whales, sperm whales, killer whales - all kinds of whales. But no such animal as a gunwhale (contrary to what some writers would have us believe).

HALF BREADTHS The beam dimensions from centreline to sheer and waterlines at each station, on the lines plan,

HALVE Two parts joined by cutting away part of each, the faying surfaces being parallel to the outer faces.

HARDWOOD Timber from the broad-leaved deciduous trees. Generally of medium to heavy weight per cubic foot.

HEEL The lower butt end of a mast, yard, gaff or sprit.

HOG (GB) The inner keel, wider than the keel, to which the garboard strakes are fastened. Same as the keelson in plywood-planked boats.

HOLDFAST NAILS (NA) *see* **'GRIPFAST NAILS'**

HORN The upper part of a stem which projects above the sheer in Norse and Shetland boats, carved (N) to a graceful curve on the inboard edge up to a narrow rounded point at the top.
INWALE The inner part of a gunwale: see gunwale.

IN WAY OF Adjacent to, alongside of, under. E.g 'Deckbeams cut out in way of kingplank', or 'Blocks fitted to hull sides in way of chainplates'.

JOGGLE Frames, floors and bulkheads may be joggled (notched) to fit the planking, as opposed to a fair curve which rests only at each land.

KABE A flat sided removeable thole as used in Shetland boats.

KEEL The main backbone member. Traditionally usually in one piece, rebated for the planking. In plywood construction the keel consists of the keelson, with the planking fitted outside, and a light outer keel or rubbing strake.

KEELBAND A half-round or flat metal band screwed to the keel to protect it.

KEELSON *see* **'HOG'**. In trad. construction the keelson may sometimes be fitted above the frames, in which case it is not a hog.

KINGPLANK The centreline deck support piece, notched into deckbeams.

LANDS/LANDINGS/LAPS/OVERLAPS The bevelled (usually) area where one plank overlaps another. The faying surface between planks. With glued plywood the width of the land is usually about three times the plank thickness in thinner ply; two or 2-1/2 times in heavier sizes (9 to 12mm-3/8 to 1/2"). Trad.: plank x 2.

LAYING OFF *see* **'LOFTING'**.

LEEBOARD A board lowered on the leeward side of a sailing craft to prevent leeway and so enable the boat to sail to windward. Usually flat on the outboard face and aerofoil-shaped inboard, to give some lift. Small craft generally have a single leeboard which is transferred to the new leeward side on tacking; cruising yachts have one each side, and raise the weather one which pivots aft. The leeboard is a little more efficient than a centreboard; a bit of a nuisance to tack; it eliminates the need for a centreboard case. It is very common in Holland and on the Thames barges; the victim of irrational prejudice elsewhere. (Except around Gloucester Massachusetts).

LINES The shape of the hull, consisting of:

•*Profile*, with vertical sections and waterlines, showing the shape of the sheerline, backbone, and buttocks.

•*Plan*, showing the sheerline and waterlines.

•*Body plan*, showing the sections and transom.

 See also **'GRID'**, **'STATIONS'**, **'SHEER'**, **'DIAGONALS'**, **'BUTTOCKS'**

The lines are drawn to the inside of the planking, or - often traditionally - to the outside (which is inconvenient for the boatbuilder, who then has to make allowance for the planking). The lines plan is also used to make calculations of displacement, stability, centre of buoyancy, prismatic coefficient, pounds-per-inch immersion etc.

LINING OUT/OFF Working out the run of each strake, and marking its position on the moulds. This is normally done before planking begins.

LOA Length overall. The length of the hull between perpendiculars, and including the stem/outer stem/false stem at sheer height. Makers of fibreglass boats sometimes include bowsprits, bumkins, mizzen booms etc in LOA figures. But usually not rudders in inboard rigged boats. This unnecessary break with tradition can be very confusing; again it is condoned - even encouraged - by the magazines, which sometimes quote Length On Deck instead. This is unacceptable; not all boats are decked, some are decked below the sheer, and some have a transom raked forward. The length of a hull is more than the **'LOD'**. Also, seeing **'LOD'** given for one boat, one then assumes that **'LOA'** given for a different boat must mean the total length - or 'Length Over Spars' - but maybe not).

LOFTING Drawing the lines of the hull full-size. This gives the exact shape of each mould, and is also used to work out the shapes of various parts, stem rebates, bevels etc.

LOGS The lower fore-and-aft timbers of a centreboard case. (May have other applications in trad. construction - generally applies to a timber roughly square in section).

LOOM GB: the part of an oar between the handle and the oarlock. NA: the part of an oar between the handle and the blade. (The British oar has a 'shaft' between oarlock and blade).

LWL Load waterline. The design waterline (DWL) at which the boat will float at her anticipated displacement.

MAST STEP *see* **'STEP'**.

MOULDS Temporary patterns cut to the shapes of the sections, set up at each station. They establish the shape of the hull as the planking is laid over them.

MOULDED The - perhaps variable - depth of a piece of wood, after cutting to its 'moulded' shape; usually perpendicular to the planking or centreline. The 'siding' is the thickness of the wood from which the piece is cut. E.g. a floor might be sided 1", fore-and-aft, and have a maximum moulded depth of 3", vertically.

OFFER UP To try a member in its place to see if it fits accurately, or needs some trimming before being permanently fitted.

OFFSETS The dimensions, taken from the lines plan, of heights (of sheer, rabbet, keel, and buttocks); the half-breadths (of the sheer and waterlines), and the diagonals. Usually expressed in feet-inches-eighths (I use sixteenths in small craft), or millimetres. The offsets are then used in lofting.

PAINTER The line used to secure a boat by the bow, or for towing. Sometimes made fast to a ring or eyebolt low on the forward face of the stem; sometimes inboard and leading through a fairlead by the stem at the sheer.

PARREL A light line holding the jaws of a gaff, gunter yard, or boom to the mast. It usually has round hardwood (or plastic) 'parrel beads' to reduce friction.

PARTNERS The hole or gap at thwart or sheer height, through which the mast passes and is supported. This may be simply a hole through the thwart, or opening aft with a gate to enable the mast to be lowered more easily.

PILLAR (GB) A stanchion.

PINTLE A rudder fitting, fastened to either hull or rudder, with a vertical pin to fit the hole in a gudgeon.

PLANK A strake, if in one piece, or a part of a strake.

PLANKING The skin of the hull, or the material it is made of.

PRAM A small boat with a transom bow.

PROFILE The side view of the hull.

QUARTER KNEE The knee joining the transom and gunwale.

QUARTER SAWN Technically, a log which is sawn into quarters, with the boards roughly radiating out from the centre, so that as far as possible the annual rings run perpendicularly across the board. In practice the sawing method is usually simplified, e.g. by starting with two or three plain-sawn boards cut across the middle of the log.

Glossary

RABBET The line of the inboard edge of the garboard, where it meets the keel, and the hood ends of the planks meet the stem, on the outboard face. (Trad.: the rabbet or rebate is also the vee-shaped cut along keel and stem into which the planks are fitted).

RAKE The angle off vertical of a mast, transom etc. Generally given in inches per foot, or mm per metre, rather than degrees, this being easier to measure in practice.

RISER *see* '**THWART RISER**'.

RIVET (n) A copper (or iron) nail, beaten to form a head over a rove.

(v) To fasten planks or other members with rivets.

ROCKER The upward curve of a keel or bottom fore-and-aft.

ROVE A slightly conical copper washer which is forced over the pointed end of a copper nail to form a rivet.

RUBBER A rubbing strake, usually at the gunwale, keel or bilge. Sometimes regarded as sacrificial and replaceable.

RUDDER CHEEKS Pieces glued to the sides of the upper narrower part of a one-piece rudder. These may be dimensioned or notched to take rudder fittings; they may extend above the transom and form a slot for the tiller. Or the sides of a pivoting rudder's case or trunk.

RUN A rather amorphous term referring to the form of the after part of the hull underwater. A racing dinghy has a flat run; a Colin Archer boat a full run; a river skiff a fine run.

SCANTLINGS The dimensions of pieces of wood in a boat.

SCARPH/SCARF Where two pieces are joined end-to-end by cutting each end to a long straight angle, the long edge of each meeting the short edge of the other. The angle is usually about 8:1, or sometimes 10:1.

SCULL (n) A high-performance oar used in racing shells.

SCULL (v) To propel a boat by means of a single oar, worked back and forth in a sculling notch. (A useful technique to learn, as a boat can be sculled in tight places where there is not room for oars; also in case of losing an oar or rowlock).

SCULLING NOTCH A half-round opening in the top of the transom to accept the loom of a sculling oar.

SHEER The line of the upper edge of the hull.

SHEERSTRAKE The upper strake of the planking.

SHELL The basic hull including backbone and planking.

SHIM A thin piece of wood (or sheet metal) used to fill a gap or to separate larger members.

SIDED The thickness of a piece of timber. See also Moulded.

SKEG A roughly triangular vertical member fitted below the keel, aft of amidships, to improve directional stability and increase lateral resistance. It usually extends to the stern, maintaining more or less the maximum depth of the keel.

SKIN The planked surface of the hull.

SNOTTER The line which holds and adjusts the heel of a sprit.

SOFTWOOD Timber from trees having needles instead of leaves: the pines, cedars etc. The annual rings are usually more clearly visible than in the hardwoods, and the wood light to medium in weight.

SPILING Measuring the width of a plank from the keel or a previous plank and thus finding the true shape when laid flat. Often achieved with the use of a wide batten clamped as close as it can fit to the curve which is to be taken off; dividers are then used to transfer this shape to the batten. Other parts such as floors and knees can be spiled to fit the planking by using a block of wood.

SPILING BATTEN A flexible batten used to draw a fair line from spiled marks.

STANCHION A vertical pillar supporting a thwart, deckbeam or other member.

STATIONS Vertical sections set perpendicular to the centreline, spaced evenly along the hull - except perhaps in the ends. The moulds are made to the shape of the sections at each station.

STEM The foremost member of the backbone, which the hood ends of the planks are fitted to. Trad.: built in one piece, rebated for the planking. In plywood construction: normally in two parts. The inner stem or apron is bevelled for the planking, which is planed flush on the forward face. The outer or false stem then covers and protects the hood ends. It is usually tapered forward to about 3/4 or 1" - 20 to 25mm wide in small craft.

STEMBAND A half-round or flat metal band screwed to the forward face of the outer stem.

STEP A hardwood block fitted to the keelson to hold the heel of the mast.

STERNPOST A vertical centreline support for the transom, not usually seen in plywood construction. The 'aft stem' in a double-ended hull.

STERNSHEETS The seat in the stern of a boat, usually extending to the transom. The term sometimes includes the aft side benches, which extend the seating forward to the aft or 'midships thwart.

STRAKE One length of planking, whether in one or more planks.

STRETCHER A board or bar fitted athwartships to give support for the feet of a rower.

TEMPLATE A pattern cut from thin plywood or board. When cut out the template is offered up to check its fit, before it is used to shape the actual piece to go into the boat.

TENDER (n) A small dinghy or pram belonging to a yacht, used for ferrying crew and gear. (Clinker plywood boats are particularly good for this purpose, because of their light weight, and ability to withstand hot and dry, as well as cold and wet conditions).

TENDER (adj) Lacking initial stability. (Which does not mean unsafe; light dories and Norwegian faerings, with low initial stability, are extraordinarily seaworthy when properly handled).

THOLES Removeable round or square pins used as rowlocks.

THWART A transverse board which ties the two sides of the boat together, usually braced to the gunwales with knees, and used as a seat.

THWART RISER A longitudinal member fitted inside the frames (if any) to support the thwarts. Usually does not extend into the ends of the hull.

TOPSIDES The side of the hull above the waterline.

TOISEAC (Scots Gaelic, pron. *toshakh*) The stem of a boat. Or, the Clan chieftain. (A non-essential item of information, but interesting .... isn't it?)

TRANSOM The flat stern member, which provides the landing for the after ends of the strakes.

TUCK The reverse, concave, turn in the lower part of a transom.

TUMBLE HOME The opposite of flare; when the topsides turn inboard towards the sheer. Usually appears aft of amidships, gradually increasing aft, and most apparent at the transom.

TURNBUTTON A small cleat, turning on a screw, used for holding down bottom boards, hatches etc. Usually of hardwood, sometimes of brass.

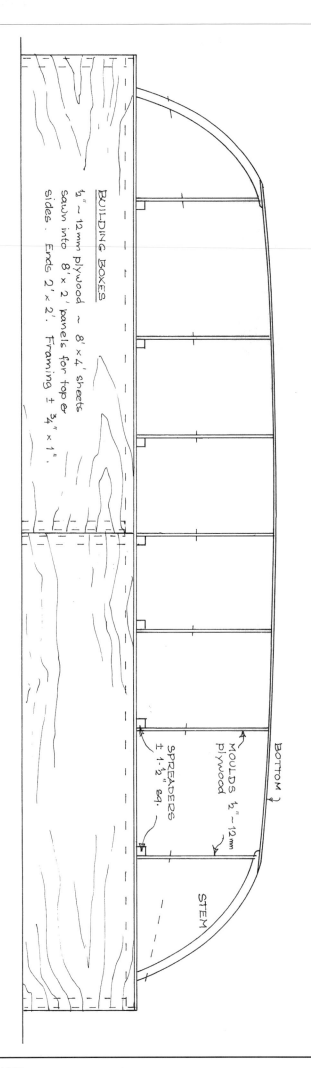

BUILDING BOXES
½" ~ 12mm plywood ~ 8' × 4' sheets
sawn into 8' × 2' panels for top &
sides. Ends 2' × 2'. Framing ± ¾" × 1".

SPREADERS
± 1-½" sq.

MOULDS ½" ~ 12mm plywood

BOTTOM

STEM

AFTERWORD

Six years after putting this book together, with yet another print run coming up, I thought there must be ways to make it better. Well, if there are, I can't see 'em.

Of course with every detail of a boat's construction there are other ways to do it; one could double the size of the book with illustrating options and alternatives. But I think such a weighty tome would be ungainly and actually less useful.

Just one item I would like to add is this substitute for the long building frame bearers. The boxes are easily made from 1/2" plywood, 2' square, using the straight "factory edge" at the top. One box can build an 8' or 10' boat; two for longer hulls. The flat top is handy for parking tools etc., and the boxes, perhaps on edge with shelves, make handy cupboards in between boat projects.

Notes